COUNTRY MUSIC

TRIVIA & FACT BOOK

Revised Edition

Compiled by
Ernie Couch

RUTLEDGE HILL PRESS
NASHVILLE, TENNESSEE

Published in Nashville, Tennessee, by Rutledge Hill Press, Inc.,
211 Seventh Avenue North, Nashville, Tennessee 37219.

Distributed in Canada by H. B. Fenn & Company, Ltd.,
34 Nixon Road, Bolton, Ontario L7E 1W2

Distributed in Australia by Millennium Books,
33 Maddox Street, Alexandria NSW 2015

Distributed in New Zealand by Tandem Press,
2 Rugby Road, Birkenhead, Auckland 10

Distributed in the United Kingdom by Verulam Publishing, Ltd.,
152a Park Street Lane, Park Street, St. Albans, Hertfordshire AL2 2AU

Typography by D&T/Bailey, Nashville, Tennessee.

Library of Congress Cataloging-in-Publication Data
Couch, Ernie, 1949–
    County music trivia & fact book/compiled by Ernie Couch. 1—
    Rev. ed.
       p.   cm.
    ISBN 1-55853-423-7
    1. Country music—Miscellanea.   I. Title.
ML3524.C63   1996
781.642—dc20   93-20504
                                                                 CIP
                                                                 MN

Printed in the United States of America
1 2 3 4 5 6 7 8 9 — 99 98 97 96

CONTENTS

To Jason and Miss Jill
and
country music fans everywhere

PREFACE

What is this phenomenon called country music that has become so popular internationally? Country music is a blend of sounds and emotion as varied as the people and cultural backgrounds from which it has evolved. It is the music of life — living, loving, winning, and losing. The ingredients include traditional Appalachian folk songs, cowboy ballads, Ozark hillbilly tunes, hoedowns, breakdowns, traditional southern gospel, black spirituals, rock, and blues, with a pinch of Cajun and Tex-Mex thrown in for good measure.

Country Music Trivia & Fact Book is the who, what, where, when, and how book of country music. Filled from cover to cover with interesting questions and answers of well-known and not-so-well-known facts about the country music world, it is designed to be informative, educational, and entertaining. Most of all, I hope you will be motivated to learn more about and continue to support this great music of the people we call country.

— Ernie Couch

ACKNOWLEDGMENTS

Special thanks to the following: John Lomax III, Dale Vinicur, Otto Kitsinger, Ronnie Pugh, Country Music Foundation; Floyd Crook, Donna Jackson, Les Leverett, Alan Mayor, Skip Jackson, Dawn Erickson, Branson Lakes Area Chamber of Commerce; Lydia Dixon Harden, *Music City News;* Irby Mandrell, Mandrell, Inc.; Heather Fambro, Liberty Records; Kim Fowler and Sandy Neese, Mercury-PolyGram Records; Mary Ann Daniel, MCA Records; Curt Campbell, Warner Brothers Records-Reprise Records; Ken Kragen, Kragen and Company; Jim Morey, Gallin-Morey & Associates; The Lee Solters Company; Patsi Cox, Gurley & Company; *Country Weekly* (magazine); *Definitive Country* (book); and *Joel Whitburn's Record Research Reports.*

1

MALE PERFORMERS

Q. In 1992 what Oklahoma town renamed its Eleventh Street, Garth Brooks Boulevard?

A. Yukon.

Q. On March 16, 1974, what *Grand Ole Opry* star gave President Richard M. Nixon yo-yo lessons at the Opry House in Nashville?

A. Roy Acuff.

Q. Country singer Marty Martin (Lecil Travis Martin) found stardom as what singing railroad hobo?

A. Boxcar Willie.

Q. Before launching his music career, what country star won fifteen consecutive bouts as a light heavyweight boxer in the Washington, D.C., area?

A. Roy Clark.

Q. Who was a dishwasher, cook, and part-time singer at the Nashville Palace when Martha Sharp signed him to Warner Brothers?

A. Randy Travis.

Q. On what ticket did singer-songwriter Stuart Hamblen run for president of the United States in 1952?

A. Prohibition Party.

Q. What stage title did Johnny Horton use when he started to appear regularly on *The Louisiana Hayride* during the mid-1950s?

A. The Singing Fisherman.

Q. *The Gayest Old Dude in Town* is the title of an album of collected works from what *Grand Ole Opry* pioneer?

A. Uncle Dave Macon.

Q. By what nickname did singer-actor Rex Allen become known during his motion picture career?

A. The Arizona Cowboy.

Q. Name the Illinois native with a rock background who became a star in 1995 with his hit video and single "Party Crowd."

A. David Lee Murphy.

Q. What is Decca recording artist Rhett Akins's unusual secondary profession?

A. He is an ordained minister.

Q. Who had multiple albums on the charts in 1994, 1995, and 1996, and is the best-selling country comedian in history?

A. Jeff Foxworthy.

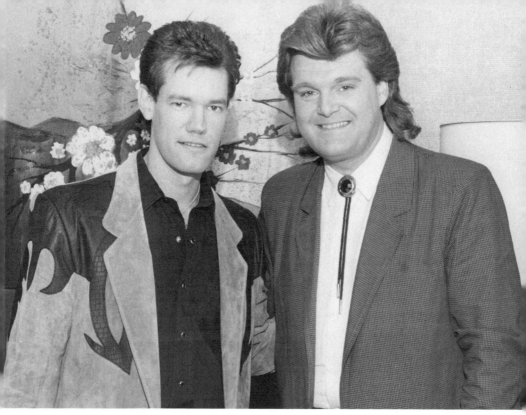

     Randy Travis and Ricky Skaggs, both representative of the "new sound of old country" music, arrived at their convergent traditional tastes from extremely divergent personal and professional backgrounds. Travis, born Randy Traywick in 1959 in Marshville, North Carolina, was a troubled teenager when he entered a talent contest at a honky-tonk in nearby Charlotte. The club's manager, Lib Hatcher, was so impressed that she petitioned the courts to put him under her guardianship. In 1981 the two moved to Nashville, where Hatcher managed the Nashville Palace and Travis washed floors, cooked, and eventually became the musical headliner there. He was signed by Warner Brothers Records in 1984; he and Hatcher were married in 1991. Ricky Skaggs, a child musical prodigy, played on Flatt and Scruggs's television show at the age of seven. When he was fifteen, he became a regular member of Ralph Stanley's band, and later worked for Emmylou Harris, the Country Gentlemen, and J. D. Crowe and the New South. He achieved true stardom in 1981 with the hit single "You May See Me Walkin'." Acknowledged as a "dazzling instrumentalist," Skaggs updated the sounds of traditional bluegrass and honky-tonk with modern rhythms and arrangements. He is married to Sharon White, of the father-daughter country gospel trio, the Whites. [Photo Courtesy of Alan Mayor]

Q. In 1987 what George Strait release became the first album ever to enter *Billboard* magazine's country chart at number one?

A. *Ocean Front Property.*

———◆———

Q. Bobby Sheridan was a pseudonym used by what recording artist early in his career?

A. Charlie Rich.

———◆———

Q. Aaron Tippin earned what type of license by age fifteen?

A. Pilot.

———◆———

Q. Where was Bobby Bare born on April 7, 1935?

A. Ironton, Ohio.

———◆———

Q. What is Carl Belew's middle name?

A. Robert.

———◆———

Q. With what label did Elton Britt record for more than twenty years?

A. RCA Records.

———◆———

Q. What recording artist was at one time a gate guard at Elvis Presley's home, Graceland, in Memphis, Tennessee?

A. Billy Swan.

———◆———

Q. What was the actual name of Oklahoma native Johnny Bond?

A. Cyrus Whitfield Bond.

Q. In what year did Garth Brooks join *The Grand Ole Opry*?

A. 1990.

———◆———

Q. Toby Keith played defensive end with what farm team of the short-lived United States Football League?

A. Oklahoma City Drillers.

———◆———

Q. In 1963 what release became Carl Butler's first million-selling single?

A. "Don't Let Me Cross Over."

———◆———

Q. Billy Ray Cyrus's first album, *Some Gave All,* sold how many copies?

A. More than eight million.

———◆———

Q. Name the birthplace of fifth-generation fiddle player, multi-instrumentalist, and singer Clinton Gregory.

A. Martinsville, Virginia.

———◆———

Q. Who appeared with Martin Delray in his video and on the single of the classic "Get Rhythm"?

A. Johnny Cash.

———◆———

Q. What recording artist has had a successful career as a cardiologist in Washington, D.C.?

A. Cleve Francis.

Q. Who had number-one hits on the Epic label with "Home" and "If the Devil Danced in Empty Pockets"?

A. Joe Diffie.

Grammy Awards
Best Country Vocal Performance, Male

1964 Roger Miller, "Dang Me"
1965 Roger Miller, "King of the Road"
1966 David Houston, "Almost Persuaded"
1967 Glen Campbell, "Gentle on My Mind"
1968 Johnny Cash, "Folsom Prison Blues"
1969 Johnny Cash, "A Boy Named Sue"
1970 Ray Price, "For the Good Times"
1971 Jerry Reed, "When You're Hot You're Hot"
1972 Charley Pride, *Charley Pride Sings Heart Songs*
       (Album)
1973 Charlie Rich, "Behind Closed Doors"
1974 Ronnie Milsap, "Please Don't Tell Me How the Story
       Ends"
1975 Willie Nelson, "Blue Eyes Crying in the Rain"
1976 Ronnie Milsap, "(I'm a) Stand by My Woman Man"
1977 Kenny Rogers, "Lucille"
1978 Willie Nelson, "Georgia on My Mind"
1979 Kenny Rogers, "The Gambler"
1980 George Jones, "He Stopped Loving Her Today"
1981 Ronnie Milsap, "(There's) No Gettin' Over Me"
1982 Willie Nelson, "Always on My Mind"
1983 Lee Greenwood, "I.O.U."
1984 Merle Haggard, "That's the Way Love Goes"
1985 Ronnie Milsap, "Lost in the Fifties Tonight"
1986 Ronnie Milsap, *Lost in the Fifties Tonight* (Album)
1987 Randy Travis, *Always and Forever* (Album)
1988 Randy Travis, "Old 8 x 10"
1989 Lyle Lovett, *Lyle Lovett and His Large Band* (Album)
1990 Vince Gill, "When I Call Your Name"
1991 Garth Brooks, *Ropin' the Wind* (Album)
1992 Vince Gill, "I Still Believe in You"
1993 Vince Gill, *I Still Believe in You* (Album)
1994 Dwight Yoakam, "Ain't That Lonely Yet"
1995 Vince Gill, "When Love Finds You"
1996 Vince Gill, "Go Rest High on That Mountain"

Q. In 1965 what rockabilly star became a regular member of *The Johnny Cash Show* tours?

A. Carl Perkins.

———◆———

Q. Although he's never had a U.S. chart record, what Irish country singer outsells all other United Kingdom-based country and folk artists?

A. Daniel O'Donnell.

———◆———

Q. In what Alabama city did Hank Williams give his last live performance on December 28, 1952?

A. Montgomery.

———◆———

Q. Who had his first big commercial breakthrough in 1969 with *Six White Horses* on the Epic label?

A. Tommy Cash.

———◆———

Q. Name the four chart hits C. W. McCall had before his 1975 pop/country smash "Convoy."

A. "Old Home Filler-up an Keep on-a-Truckin Cafe," "Wolf Creek Pass," "Classified," and "Black Bear Road."

———◆———

Q. In 1962 what singer had the million-selling album *Modern Sounds in Country and Western Music* on the ABC Records label?

A. Ray Charles.

———◆———

Q. What is Doug Stone's real surname?

A. Brooks.

Q. Buffalo, New York, is the hometown of what recording artist who had a Top-10 hit single with "What a Way to Go"?

A. Ray Kennedy.

---◆---

Q. As a child, James Blundell had an offer to become a member of what internationally renowned choir?

A. Vienna Boys Choir.

---◆---

Q. Primarily known as a white soul singer, what native of Fort Worth, Texas, received a Grammy nomination for his 1993 duet with Tanya Tucker?

A. Delbert McClinton, with "Tell Me about It."

---◆---

Q. What West Virginia town is the birthplace of Billy Edd Wheeler?

A. Whitesville.

---◆---

Q. What country vocalist noted for his use of falsetto served on the USS *Chilton* during World War II?

A. Slim Whitman.

---◆---

Q. Who wrote numerous country hits and produces superstar Alan Jackson?

A. Keith Stegall.

---◆---

Q. Lee Roy Parnell is a native of what Texas city?

A. Abilene.

Q. When was Canadian singer-guitarist Ronnie Prophet born?

A. December 26, 1937.

---◆---

Q. What old-time singer, fiddler, and banjo and guitar picker died in 1946 of blood poisoning caused by an infected neck boil?

A. Riley Puckett.

---◆---

Q. What performer was born Edward Thomas on November 27, 1944, in Brooklyn, New York?

A. Eddie Rabbitt.

---◆---

Q. What 1994 hit single for Tim McGraw drew charges by Native Americans of promoting negative stereotypes?

A. "Indian Outlaw."

---◆---

Q. What is the actual name of Hank Williams's illegitimate daughter, Jett Williams?

A. Cathy Yvonne Stone.

---◆---

Q. What actress did Clint Black marry in October 1991?

A. Lisa Hartman.

---◆---

Q. In what year did Buck Owens have his hit single "I've Got a Tiger by the Tail"?

A. 1965.

Oklahoma native Vince Gill first came to public attention as a member of country rock band Pure Prairie League. He followed that with a stint in Emmylou Harris's band, then launched a solo career in 1984. He didn't strike paydirt immediately, but he soared with "When I Call Your Name" in 1990, winning "Single of the Year" from the CMA, in addition to a Grammy. As of 1996 he had won more CMA honors than anyone in history and had added five more Grammys. A remarkable songwriter and wonderful singer, Gill also is a vastly talented guitarist, widely acknowledged as one of the most accommodating performers in Nashville for his many charitable efforts. [VICTORIA PEARSON PHOTO PROVIDED BY MCA NASHVILLE]

Q. What singer-songwriter was born in Sunflower County, Mississippi, on January 23, 1940?

A. John Bright "Johnny" Russell.

◆

Q. Although he was raised in Bakersfield, California, where was Ronnie Sessions born on December 7, 1948?

A. Henrietta, Oklahoma.

Q. Bill Browder, a native of Humbolt, Tennessee, has what stage name?

A. T. G. Sheppard.

Q. In 1983 what artist had a hit single about a ghostly meeting with Hank Williams entitled "The Ride"?

A. David Allan Coe.

Q. With what title did Gene Autry start billing himself over radio station KVOO in Tulsa, Oklahoma, in 1930?

A. Oklahoma's Singing Cowboy.

Q. In 1963 what was Roy Clark's first hit on Capitol Records?

A. "Tips of My Fingers."

Q. Who used the stage name Tommy Dean from Abilene on television in Houston, Texas?

A. Tommy Overstreet.

Q. What was Georgia-born John Berry's 1993 debut single and video with Liberty Records?

A. "She's Got a Mind of Her Own."

Q. Who was Johnny Cash's first wife?

A. Vivian Liberto.

Q. What performer, born in Versailles, Kentucky, on August 11, 1946, worked as a mortician for six years?

A. John Conlee.

◆

Q. Who sang the classic 1964 hit single "The Race Is On"?

A. George Jones.

◆

Q. Where was Mark Chesnutt born on September 6, 1963?

A. Beaumont, Texas.

◆

Q. In 1947 who headlined the first country show to play New York's Carnegie Hall?

A. Ernest Tubb.

◆

Q. Who is tallest among Alan Jackson, Billy Dean, and Toby Keith?

A. All are six feet, four inches.

◆

Q. What is Floridian Slim Whitman's full name?

A. Otis Dewey Whitman Jr.

◆

Q. What 1959 single by Billy "Crash" Craddock was a hit in Australia?

A. "Don't Destroy Me."

◆

Q. Which Beatle recorded country chart single "Sally G" in Music City?

A. Paul McCartney.

In 1992 Kentucky native Billy Ray Cyrus soared to national attention with his "Achy Breaky Heart" video and single. A new dance craze was born and within a few weeks fans were packing country music dance halls to do the Achy Breaky. [BY PERMISSION OF MERCURY/POLYGRAM RECORDS]

Q. Who was the masked man who consistently enjoyed country hits on Sun Records between 1979 and 1982?

A. Orion, born Jimmy Ellis in 1945 in Alabama. He wore the mask hoping people might think he was Elvis.

◆

Q. During what years did Country Music Hall of Famer James H. "Jimmie" Davis serve as governor of Louisiana?

A. 1944–48 and 1960–64.

◆

Q. What Texas-born performer was at one time an employee of the Georgia State Board of Probation?

A. Mac Davis.

◆

Q. What country star of the 1960s and 1970s became a sausage entrepreneur?

A. Jimmy Dean.

Q. What was the full name given by Garth and Sandy Brooks to their first child, who was born on July 8, 1992, at Baptist Hospital in Nashville?

A. Taylor Mayne Pearl Brooks.

———◆———

Q. How tall is Little Jimmy Dickens?

A. Four feet, eleven inches.

———◆———

Q. At what age did David Houston win a guest spot on *The Louisiana Hayride*?

A. Twelve.

———◆———

Q. What soulful New Orleans vocalist recorded with Linda Ronstadt and the Rolling Stones and had a country hit with his 1993 version of "The Grand Tour"?

A. Aaron Neville, of the Neville Brothers.

———◆———

Q. What singer-songwriter was born Warner McPherson on April 2, 1938?

A. Warner Mack.

———◆———

Q. During the program inducting him into *The Grand Ole Opry* on November 28, 1992, what performer made a faux pas with his "old farts" statement?

A. Marty Stuart.

———◆———

Q. What was Stonewall Jackson's massive 1959 crossover hit?

A. "Waterloo."

(L to r) Cajun singers Jo-el Sonnier, Eddy Raven, Jimmy C. Newman, and Doug Kershaw appearing as guests on Ralph Emery's Nashville Now *television show.* [PHOTO BY ALAN MAYOR]

Cajun Music

Cajun music is the indigenous music of southwestern Louisiana which was settled by French colonials from Acadia (Nova Scotia) in the mid-eighteenth century. (The word *Cajun* is a corrupted form of *Acadian.*) Their isolationist life in the swampy Louisiana frontiers preserved their culture in much the same way as the remote mountain regions of the Ozarks and the Appalachians held those folkways intact. The Acadians brought with them their folksongs and their fiddles, but it was the addition of the diatonic accordion in the mid-to-late 1800s that transformed Cajun music and gave it its recognizable and distinctive sound. Cajun music was first recorded in the late 1920s, but it was Harry Choates's 1946 recording of "Jole Blon" that introduced the style into the country music mainstream.

Q. What truck-driving single was an international million seller for C. W. McCall?

A. "Convoy."

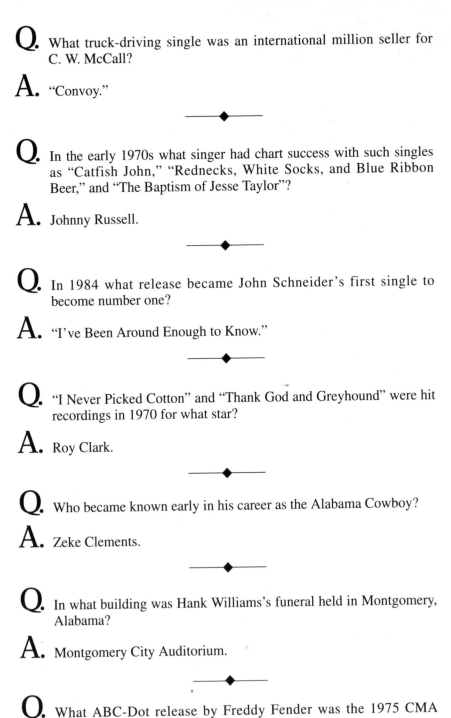

Q. In the early 1970s what singer had chart success with such singles as "Catfish John," "Rednecks, White Socks, and Blue Ribbon Beer," and "The Baptism of Jesse Taylor"?

A. Johnny Russell.

Q. In 1984 what release became John Schneider's first single to become number one?

A. "I've Been Around Enough to Know."

Q. "I Never Picked Cotton" and "Thank God and Greyhound" were hit recordings in 1970 for what star?

A. Roy Clark.

Q. Who became known early in his career as the Alabama Cowboy?

A. Zeke Clements.

Q. In what building was Hank Williams's funeral held in Montgomery, Alabama?

A. Montgomery City Auditorium.

Q. What ABC-Dot release by Freddy Fender was the 1975 CMA Single of the Year?

A. "Before the Next Teardrop Falls."

Q. Whigham, Georgia, is the birthplace of what hit-making male country star?

A. Daryle Singletary.

———◆———

Q. In 1948 what *Grand Ole Opry* star was the Republican Party's candidate for governor of Tennessee?

A. Roy Acuff.

———◆———

Q. What Oklahoman became the first new breakthrough country artist for 1995 with his single "Old Enough to Know Better"?

A. Wade Hayes.

———◆———

Q. Waylon Jennings, Willie Nelson, Johnny Cash, and Kris Kristofferson collaborated on what 1985 hit album?

A. *Highwayman.*

———◆———

Q. With whom did Red Foley costar on the 1939 radio program *Avalon Times*?

A. Red Skelton.

———◆———

Q. What country music veteran died on January 2, 1974, from a heart attack he suffered while arranging bail for one of his band members who was being held in the Metro Nashville jail?

A. Tex Ritter.

———◆———

Q. Where did Red Steagall study animal husbandry?

A. West Texas State University.

Q. Following high school, Tennessee Ernie Ford studied music at what institution?

A. Cincinnati Conservatory of Music.

———◆———

Q. John Michael Montgomery was born and raised in what Kentucky county?

A. Jessamine.

———◆———

Q. What cut from David Frizzell's album *The Family's Fine, but This One's Mine* was a number-one hit?

A. "I'm Gonna Hire a Wino to Decorate Our Home."

———◆———

Q. Because his dad worked for the state department, his family lived in Italy, Nigeria, the Philippines, and Saudi Arabia. Name this hit country writer and recording artist.

A. Marcus Hummon.

———◆———

Q. During the mid-1970s, who had country hits with such pop songs as "Yellow Ribbon," "Afternoon Delight," and "Living Next Door to Alice"?

A. Johnny Carver.

———◆———

Q. Tejano sensation Emilio first crossed over to the country charts with his 1995 hit "It's Not the End of the World." What's his last name?

A. Navaria.

———◆———

Q. What color are George Strait's eyes?

A. Blue.

Willie Nelson as a bass player with Ray Price's Cherokee Cowboys in the early 1960s. (l to r) Ray Price, Willie Nelson, and fiddler Buddy Spicher. [PHOTO COURTESY OF SKIP JACKSON]

Q. Who had two Top-10 singles in 1965 with "Green, Green Grass of Home," and "Skid Row Joe"?

A. Porter Wagoner.

◆

Q. In 1949 what country and western performer surpassed Bing Crosby and Frank Sinatra in a pop vocalist poll taken by *Billboard* magazine?

A. James Clarence "Jimmy" Wakely.

◆

Q. Who wrote and recorded the first hit version of "Amarillo by Morning" in 1974?

A. Terry Stafford.

Q. How many CMA awards did Johnny Cash receive in 1969?

A. Five.

———◆———

Q. What singer recorded the big 1950 hit "If You've Got the Money I've Got the Time"?

A. Lefty Frizzell.

———◆———

Q. What was John Berry's first number-one single?

A. "Your Love Amazes Me."

———◆———

Q. During the 1960s what artist became known as the Jolly Green Giant?

A. Jack Greene.

———◆———

Q. What performer took his stage name from the names of an Arkansas town and a Texas town?

A. Conway Twitty.

———◆———

Q. What was Marty Robbins's biggest all-time single, which was released in 1959?

A. "El Paso."

———◆———

Q. Who has been called the Father of Country Music?

A. Jimmie Rodgers.

Q. What was Red Foley's real name?

A. Clyde Julian Foley.

---◆---

Q. What was Lee Greenwood's first single on the MCA label?

A. "It Turns Me Inside Out."

---◆---

Q. What country music legend was released from San Quentin Prison in 1960 after being paroled for attempted burglary?

A. Merle Haggard.

---◆---

Q. Olive Hill, Kentucky, is the birthplace of what country singer-songwriter?

A. Tom T. Hall.

---◆---

Q. In what year did John Conlee join *The Grand Ole Opry*?

A. 1981.

---◆---

Q. In 1992 what longtime *Grand Ole Opry* member ran for a seat in the Tennessee state senate?

A. Charlie Walker.

---◆---

Q. What actress did Johnny Lee marry on February 14, 1982?

A. Charlene Tilton.

Q. In 1968 what performer had country chart hits with "Another Place, Another Time" and "What's Made Milwaukee Famous (Has Made a Loser out of Me)"?

A. Jerry Lee Lewis.

Q. What hit single by Slim Whitman topped the British pop charts for eleven consecutive weeks in 1955?

A. "Rose Marie."

Q. How did Bryan White get his start in music?

A. The young Asylum Records star played drums in his father's band.

Q. In 1958 what country singer-songwriter won a Rhodes scholarship to Oxford University in England?

A. Kris Kristofferson.

Q. In 1965 who had his first number-one single with "Girl on the Billboard"?

A. Del Reeves.

Q. What award-winning California writer-artist was an original member of the Nitty Gritty Dirt Band?

A. Jackson Browne.

Q. In the early 1960s, where did Freddy Fender serve three years for a conviction on drug possession?

A. Angola State Penitentiary, Louisiana.

Q. At what age did Tim McGraw learn that his biological father was major league baseball pitcher Tug McGraw?

A. Eleven.

Q. Goebel Reeves claims to have been the one who taught what performer how to yodel?

A. Jimmie Rodgers.

Q. In 1991 what country star was shot four times by robbers outside his Nashville hotel room?

A. Tracy Lawrence.

Q. What male country star worked as a concert promoter in Texas before getting a Top-5 hit with "Reno" in 1993?

A. Doug Supernaw.

Q. What is Buck Owens's real name?

A. Alvid Edgar Owens Jr.

Q. What 1980 release from George Jones earned him a Grammy for Best Male Country Vocal Performance?

A. "He Stopped Loving Her Today."

Q. Following Marvin Rainwater's 1956 signing with MGM, what song, written and recorded by him, was his only one to be a million seller?

A. "Gonna Find Me a Bluebird."

Q. How old was Merle Kilgore when he became a DJ on radio station KENT in Shreveport, Louisiana?

A. Sixteen.

Q. What bluegrass singer and picker was born near Waynesboro, Virginia, on May 23, 1925?

A. Mac Wiseman.

Q. What is Grandpa Jones's full name?

A. Louis Marshall Jones.

Q. Who had such hit singles as "Two Less Lonely People," "Lonely Street," and "Me and My Broken Heart"?

A. Rex Allen Jr.

Q. What is Bill Anderson's nickname?

A. Whispering Bill.

Q. In 1984 what RCA release became Eddy Raven's first number-one single?

A. "I Got Mexico."

Q. Born on Christmas Day 1954, Steve Wariner was given what middle name?

A. Noel.

CMA Male Vocalist of the Year

1967	Jack Greene	1982	Ricky Skaggs
1968	Glen Campbell	1983	Lee Greenwood
1969	Johnny Cash	1984	Lee Greenwood
1970	Merle Haggard	1985	George Strait
1971	Charley Pride	1986	George Strait
1972	Charley Pride	1987	Randy Travis
1973	Charlie Rich	1988	Randy Travis
1974	Ronnie Milsap	1989	Ricky Van Shelton
1975	Waylon Jennings	1990	Clint Black
1976	Ronnie Milsap	1991	Vince Gill
1977	Ronnie Milsap	1992	Vince Gill
1978	Don Williams	1993	Vince Gill
1979	Kenny Rogers	1994	Vince Gill
1980	George Jones	1995	Alan Jackson
1981	George Jones		

Q. In 1975 "Love in the Hot Afternoon" was what artist's first Top-5 hit with Capitol Records?

A. Gene Watson.

◆

Q. What country performer is said to have been given his nickname because of his southpaw punch?

A. Lefty Frizzell.

◆

Q. To whom did Waylon Jennings give up his seat on the 1959 ill-fated flight that took the lives of all on board, including Buddy Holly?

A. J. P. Richardson (the Big Bopper).

◆

Q. "I.O.U.," "Somebody's Gonna Love You," and "Going, Going, Gone" were all crossover hits for what country artist in 1983?

A. Lee Greenwood.

Q. What singer recorded "Lovesick Blues" on the Decca label almost a decade before Hank Williams?

A. Rex Griffin.

———◆———

Q. Whom did Merle Haggard marry on October 7, 1978?

A. Leona Williams.

———◆———

Q. What artist was born in Littlefield, Texas, on June 15, 1937?

A. Waylon Jennings.

———◆———

Q. On what type of naval vessel did Stonewall Jackson serve during the early 1950s?

A. Submarine.

———◆———

Q. Who had a Top-10 hit with "Silent Treatment" and a number-one hit with "Fire & Smoke"?

A. Earl Thomas Conley.

———◆———

Q. What was Roy Acuff's middle name?

A. Claxton.

———◆———

Q. In what year did David Houston have his monster hit "Almost Persuaded"?

A. 1966.

———◆———

Q. Where was William Smith "Bill" Monroe born on September 13, 1911?

A. Rosine, Kentucky.

Q. On what label did Roger Miller have his first million seller, "Dang Me"?

A. Smash.

———◆———

Q. In 1963 what single on the Epic label became David Houston's first national hit?

A. "Mountain of Love."

———◆———

Q. Who was the first country artist to sign with Frank Sinatra's Reprise label?

A. Del Reeves.

———◆———

Q. What was Lefty Frizzell's actual name?

A. William Orville Frizzell.

———◆———

Q. On his mother's side of the family, Neal McCoy traces his ethnic heritage to what Pacific Rim nation?

A. The Philippines.

———◆———

Q. "I Overlooked and Orchid" and "City Lights" were both chart toppers for what artist in 1974 and 1975?

A. Mickey Gilley.

———◆———

Q. In the late 1950s Vern Gosdin performed gospel music over what Birmingham, Alabama, radio station?

A. WVOK.

Q. Who had three Top-20 hit singles, "Diane," "The Last Cowboy Song," and "Girls, Women, and Ladies," with MCA Records in 1980?

A. Ed Bruce.

◆

Q. Who recorded the 1967 hit single "Pop a Top"?

A. Jim Ed Brown.

◆

Q. What was Hank Williams's only hit single in the pop charts in 1952, reaching number twenty?

A. "Jambalaya (On the Bayou)."

◆

Q. What country artist took his stage name from the brand of amplifier he used?

A. Freddie Fender.

◆

Q. In 1969 who became the first American country artist to record a complete album of Canadian songs?

A. George Hamilton IV.

◆

Q. Who has been called the Country Caruso?

A. Johnny Bush.

◆

Q. Delight, Arkansas, is acknowledged as the birthplace of what performer?

A. Glen Campbell.

When Alan Jackson decided to move from his native Newnan, Georgia, home to Nashville to pursue a career in country music, his wife, Denise, a flight attendant, encountered Glen Campbell by chance at the Atlanta airport and asked him his advice. Campbell gave her his business card and told her to have Alan contact his publishing company once they arrived in Nashville. This offer eventually led to a regular job as a staff songwriter with the publisher and bookings across the country with Campbell's organization. Jackson signed with Arista Records in 1989 and his first hit single was "Blue Blooded Woman." Here in the Real World, *his first album, produced four consecutive number-one singles. He became a member of* The Grand Ole Opry *in 1991.* [PHOTO COURTESY OF ALAN MAYOR]

Q. Under what stage name did Goebel Reeves perform?

A. The Texas Drifter.

◆

Q. In 1956 what was Johnny Horton's first national hit single?

A. "Honky-Tonk Man."

Q. On what Montana mountain did Hank Williams Jr. almost lose his life in a hiking accident on August 8, 1975?

A. Ajax Mountain.

Q. Whom did Chet Atkins describe as being "the greatest one-man show I've seen"?

A. Ronnie Prophet.

Q. What is Emilio's date of birth and what was the name of his first album?

A. He was born August 23, 1963, and his first album was called *Emilio y Rio*.

Q. Who was the first American country artist to perform in Russia?

A. George Hamilton IV.

Q. Which two Grammy Award-winning artists recorded singles with Tejano accordion virtuoso Flaco Jimenez?

A. Dwight Yoakam, and the Mavericks.

Q. Who has belonged to a famous rock/country band, scored movies and television films, and dueled on banjo with Steve Martin?

A. John McEuen.

Q. Who had a Top-10 hit on the Columbia label in 1949 with "But I'll Go Chasin' Women"?

A. Stuart Hamblen.

Q. What baseball great originally dubbed Roy Acuff "the King of Country Music"?

A. Dizzy Dean.

———◆———

Q. Born in Wilcox, Arizona, on December 31, 1920, who was the last of the motion picture singing cowboys?

A. Rex Allen.

———◆———

Q. In 1959 what single became Johnny Horton's first number-one hit?

A. "When It's Springtime in Alaska (It's Forty Below)."

———◆———

Q. What Harlan County, Kentucky, native, known for his renditions of authentic American folksongs, was a regular on *The National Barn Dance* during the 1930s and 1940s?

A. Doctor Howard "Doc" Hopkins.

———◆———

Q. What product did Carl Smith sell to earn money to purchase his first guitar?

A. Flower seeds.

———◆———

Q. George Jones recorded a duet, "A Stranger in the House," with what English rock singer?

A. Elvis Costello.

———◆———

Q. What performer, born in Greensboro, North Carolina, on June 16, 1939, became known as Mr. Country Rock?

A. Billy "Crash" Craddock.

Q. When he was born in Liverpool, Nova Scotia, on May 9, 1914, Hank Snow was given what full name?

A. Clarence Eugene Snow.

———◆———

Q. Otis W. "Joe" Maphis was an uncle to what singing sisters?

A. The Mandrells.

———◆———

Q. Who was known as the Dixie Dewdrop?

A. Uncle Dave Macon.

———◆———

Q. Although it was released in 1984, what single went number one for Mel McDaniel in 1985?

A. "Baby's Got Her Blue Jeans On."

———◆———

Q. What performer started disguising himself as an old-timer while he was still in his twenties?

A. Grandpa Jones.

———◆———

Q. Skeets McDonald was a longtime performer on what West Coast program?

A. *Town Hall Party.*

———◆———

Q. In the mid-1980s what recording artist became mayor of Ouray, Colorado?

A. C. W. McCall (William Fries).

Q. Who was the first country entertainer to get MTV exposure for a video clip?

A. Ronnie Milsap, for "She Loves My Car."

———◆———

Q. What was Skyland Scotty's actual name?

A. Scott Wiseman.

———◆———

Q. What singer-songwriter attended Memphis State University on a boxing partial scholarship?

A. Dickey Lee.

———◆———

Q. Where did Claude King attend college?

A. University of Idaho.

———◆———

Q. Whose recording of "Shenandoah Waltz" sold some three million copies on the King label?

A. Clyde Moody.

———◆———

Q. In January 1993 who performed the national anthem at Super Bowl XXVII?

A. Garth Brooks.

———◆———

Q. Where was Merle Haggard born on April 6, 1937?

A. Bakersfield, California.

Q. "(Old Dogs, Children, and) Watermelon Wine" and "Ravishing Ruby" were hits for what artist?

A. Tom T. Hall.

———◆———

Q. What was Roger Miller's middle name?

A. Dean.

———◆———

Q. Prior to pursuing a full-time music career, Bill Anderson had trained for a career in what field?

A. Journalism.

———◆———

Q. In 1984 what single became Gary Morris's first number-one hit?

A. "Baby Bye Bye."

———◆———

Q. Where was Australian country star Tex Morton born in 1916?

A. Nelson, New Zealand.

———◆———

Q. Who earned a nocturnal nickname in the early 1930s from playing piano and singing at night in houses of ill-repute in Houston, Texas?

A. Moon Mullican.

———◆———

Q. Who became known as the Baron of Bakersfield?

A. Buck Owens.

———◆———

Q. For what truck-driving hit single is Dave Dudley best known?

A. "Six Days on the Road."

Q. Who had number-one singles in the mid-1970s with "Thinkin' of a Rendezvous" and "It Couldn't Have Been Any Better"?

A. Johnny Duncan.

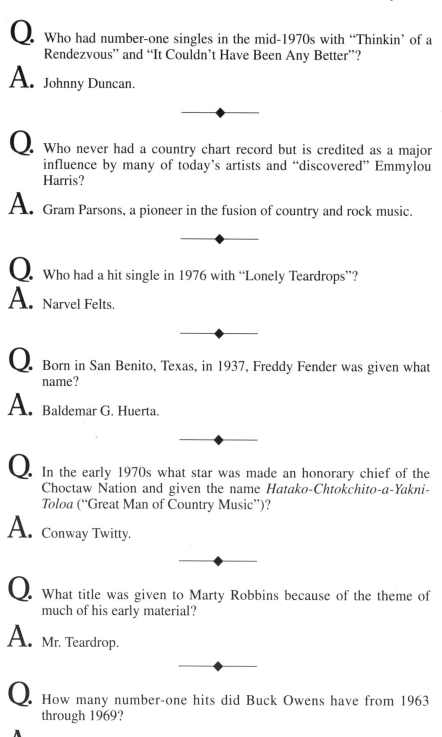

Q. Who never had a country chart record but is credited as a major influence by many of today's artists and "discovered" Emmylou Harris?

A. Gram Parsons, a pioneer in the fusion of country and rock music.

Q. Who had a hit single in 1976 with "Lonely Teardrops"?

A. Narvel Felts.

Q. Born in San Benito, Texas, in 1937, Freddy Fender was given what name?

A. Baldemar G. Huerta.

Q. In the early 1970s what star was made an honorary chief of the Choctaw Nation and given the name *Hatako-Chtokchito-a-Yakni-Toloa* ("Great Man of Country Music")?

A. Conway Twitty.

Q. What title was given to Marty Robbins because of the theme of much of his early material?

A. Mr. Teardrop.

Q. How many number-one hits did Buck Owens have from 1963 through 1969?

A. Nineteen.

Q. Released on the Mercury label in 1962, what was James O'Gwynn's biggest hit?

A. "My Name Is Mud."

Q. Before hitting it big with "Thinkin' Problem" in 1994, David Ball had late-1980s chart records such as "Steppin' Out" for what label?

A. RCA.

Q. What is Ohio-born Johnny PayCheck's actual name?

A. Donald Eugene Lytle.

Q. Pee Wee King was originally trained for a career in what profession?

A. Drafting.

Q. What recording of a Ray Price classic was Jerry Lee Lewis's first release on the Sun label?

A. "Crazy Arms."

Q. During the 1960s what performer was mayor of McLellan, Florida?

A. Hank Locklin.

Q. During his early days in Nashville, Kris Kristofferson worked as a janitor at what record company's studio?

A. Columbia Records.

Q. Under what pseudonym did Johnny PayCheck record some rocka-billy cuts in the early 1960s?

A. Donny Young.

———◆———

Q. Singer-songwriter William Clarence "Bill" Phillips joined the cast of what Miami, Florida, radio program in 1955?

A. *Old Southern Jamboree.*

———◆———

Q. Known as "the Baron" of country music, what Maine native is best remembered for "A Tombstone Every Mile" and "Six Times a Day"?

A. Dick Curless, who recorded his last album, *Traveling Through*, just before his untimely death in 1995.

Australian Country Music and Slim Dusty

Although the pioneering Australian country musicians were heavily influenced by their contemporary American counterparts, they also searched for their own identities in the unique Australian environment and experience. As was true in the United States, radio played an important role in acquainting Australia's scattered rural population with the music of their earliest stars, including Smoky Dawson, Slim Dusty, Tex Morton, Gordon Parsons, and Buddy Williams.

———◆———

David Gordon Kirkpatrick, who by age eleven was known as Slim Dusty, is considered to be Australia's most legendary country star. In 1946 he wrote his signature tune, "When the Rain Tumbles Down in July." The song, which reflected Slim's intimate understanding of his native land, was a departure from the imitative American cowboy music that had become popular. The song was based on the real-life hardships that his family and neighbors suffered through during the great Australian floods of 1946 and did much to establish a separate Australian country music identity.

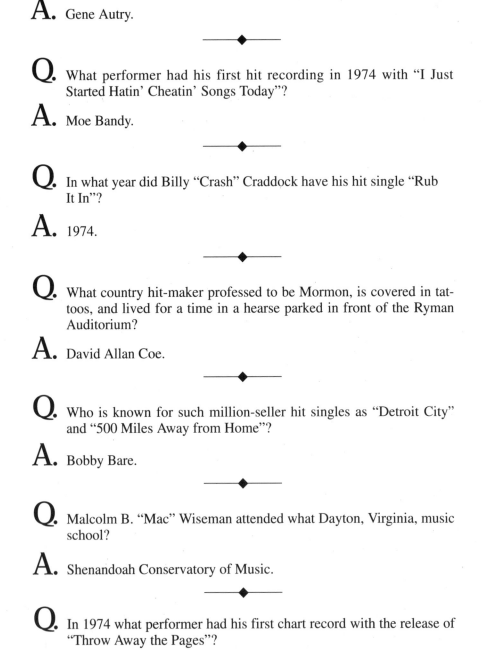

Q. What singing cowboy was born at Tioga, Texas, on September 29, 1907?

A. Gene Autry.

Q. What performer had his first hit recording in 1974 with "I Just Started Hatin' Cheatin' Songs Today"?

A. Moe Bandy.

Q. In what year did Billy "Crash" Craddock have his hit single "Rub It In"?

A. 1974.

Q. What country hit-maker professed to be Mormon, is covered in tattoos, and lived for a time in a hearse parked in front of the Ryman Auditorium?

A. David Allan Coe.

Q. Who is known for such million-seller hit singles as "Detroit City" and "500 Miles Away from Home"?

A. Bobby Bare.

Q. Malcolm B. "Mac" Wiseman attended what Dayton, Virginia, music school?

A. Shenandoah Conservatory of Music.

Q. In 1974 what performer had his first chart record with the release of "Throw Away the Pages"?

A. Randy Barlow.

Q. "In the Jailhouse Now," "Love, Love, Love," and "I Don't Care" were all number-one hits for what recording artist in 1955?

A. Webb Pierce.

———◆———

Q. What early *Hee Haw* regular was known as the Round Mound of Sound?

A. Kenny Price.

———◆———

Q. Who had the hits "Okie from Muskogee" and "The Fightin' Side of Me"?

A. Merle Haggard.

———◆———

Q. Which NASCAR driver sported David Lee Murphy's *Out with a Bang* album cover on the back of his car at the 1996 Daytona 500?

A. Jeff Purvis.

———◆———

Q. Who achieved a number-one hit in the country charts with "Fraulein"?

A. Bobby Helms.

———◆———

Q. "Easy Loving" was a megahit for what performer in 1971?

A. Freddie Hart.

———◆———

Q. Known for such singles as "Small Town Saturday Night" and "Past the Point of Rescue," Hal Ketchum was born in what New York town?

A. Greenwich.

Q. What Atlanta, Texas, native had a number-one hit single with "Sticks and Stones"?

A. Tracy Lawrence.

◆

Q. Who became known as the Cherokee Cowboy?

A. Ray Price.

◆

Q. What was Charley Pride's first single with RCA, which was released in December 1965?

A. "The Snakes Crawl at Night."

◆

Q. Beaumont, Texas, native Clay Walker holds what distinction at his label, Giant Records?

A. He was the first individual artist on the country division of the label to attain gold and platinum sales.

◆

Q. In the late 1960s what single brought Henson Cargill to national attention?

A. "Skip a Rope."

◆

Q. What performer had open-heart surgery in January 1970?

A. Marty Robbins.

◆

Q. For what release did Ray Price receive his only Grammy in 1971?

A. "For the Good Times."

◆

Q. Whom did Don Gibson marry in June 1967?

A. Bobbi Patterson.

The release of Georgia-born Travis Tritt's first single, "Country Club," came in November 1989. A solid string of hit singles, albums, and videos followed. In February 1992 Travis was inducted as the then youngest member into The Grand Ole Opry. [BY PERMISSION OF WARNER BROS. RECORDS]

Q. In what Atlanta, Georgia, suburb did Bill Anderson attend high school?

A. Avondale.

———◆———

Q. What were Porter Wagoner's two number-one hits as a solo artist?

A. "A Satisfied Mind" (1955) and "Misery Loves Company" (1962).

———◆———

Q. To what Texas city did Willie Nelson relocate in 1972?

A. Austin.

———◆———

Q. What 1983 John Anderson hit refers to Charlotte Johnson?

A. "Swingin'."

Q. How many number-one songs did Freddie Hart have?

A. Six.

◆

Q. With something over eighty-five million units sold, what artist has the most record sales for country music?

A. Eddy Arnold.

◆

Q. What entertainer was the first to be married at home plate in the Astrodome in Houston, Texas?

A. Doug Kershaw.

◆

Q. What modern-day singing cowboy won the 1976 world championship in bareback bronco riding?

A. Chris LeDoux.

◆

Q. What country performer is named for a Confederate general?

A. Stonewall Jackson.

◆

Q. What is the stage name of Texan Hubert Neal McGaughey Jr.?

A. Neal McCoy.

◆

Q. "I'll Never Get Out of This World Alive" was one of what artist's last releases before his death in 1953?

A. Hank Williams.

◆

Q. How tall is Capitol/Nashville chart artist Trace Adkins?

A. Six feet, seven inches.

Q. What was the title of Radney Foster's debut album on the Arista label?

A. *Del Rio, TX 1959.*

Q. Where was Tennessee Ernie Ford born on February 13, 1919?

A. Bristol, Tennessee.

Q. In 1959 what Mercury recording of a J. P. "Big Bopper" Richardson composition became George Jones's first number-one hit?

A. "White Lightning."

Q. Which Texas singer scored a career breakthrough with a song called "Keeper of the Stars"?

A. Tracy Byrd.

Q. "Mexican Joe" and "Bimbo" were early hits on the Abbott label for what artist?

A. Jim Reeves.

Q. What performer was born on March 20, 1937, in Atlanta, Georgia?

A. Jerry Reed.

Q. What was the name of Ray Charles's 1984 album that featured many of the top stars in country music?

A. *Friendship.*

Q. What is Roy Clark's middle name?

A. Linwood.

Canada's Wilf Carter (Montana Slim)

Born in 1904, Wilf Carter was a cowboy who was raised in Nova Scotia's ranch country, worked as a ranch hand, and traveled the rodeo circuit as a chuck wagon racer, wild-cow milker, and wild-horse rider. Also an itinerant picker and singer, Carter was inspired by a vaudeville Swiss-style yodeler he once heard as a side attraction at a performance of the play *Uncle Tom's Cabin*. When Wilf was hired soon afterwards by the Canadian Pacific Railways to provide entertainment on trail rides through the Canadian Rockies, he spent hours practicing and perfecting the yodel.

In 1932 Carter was signed by RCA Victor's Canadian division. His first record for RCA, in 1933, was a yodeling song that he composed called "Swiss Moonlight Lullaby." He worked on radio stations in Calgary and Vancouver, then moved to New York for a CBS radio show. It was around this time that CBS announcer Bert Parks introduced him as "Montana Slim," a nickname that he liked and decided to keep. Also known as the Cowboy Yodeler, for years Carter was Canada's top country entertainer. He wrote hundreds of songs, most of which, like "I'm Hittin' the Trail," were based on western themes.

Q. At what age did Del Reeves have his own radio show in North Carolina?

A. Twelve.

————◆————

Q. What did the initials in O. B. McClinton's name stand for?

A. Obie Burnett.

————◆————

Q. What is Dickey Lee's real surname?

A. Lipscomb.

Q. Who had the World War II million-selling hit record "There's a Star-Spangled Banner Waving Somewhere"?

A. Elton Britt.

Q. What single by John D. Loudermilk on RCA was a hit in both the United States and Britain during the winter of 1961–62?

A. "Language of Love."

Q. Who became known during the 1940s as the Hillbilly Waltz King?

A. Clyde Moody.

Q. In addition to the re-release of "There Won't Be Anymore," what two new releases by Charlie Rich also went to the top of the charts in 1973?

A. "Behind Closed Doors" and "The Most Beautiful Girl."

Q. What was Tex Ritter's actual name?

A. Woodward Maurice Ritter.

Q. At age seventeen Buck Owens started performing with a country band on what Mesa, Arizona, radio station?

A. KTYL.

Q. What 1975 single by Ray Stevens won a Grammy for Best Arrangement Accompanying a Vocalist?

A. "Misty."

Q. What country star got his nickname Bocephus from a puppet in a Rod Brasfield routine?

A. Hank Williams Jr.

Q. Where did singer-songwriter Wynn Stewart open his own club in the early 1960s?

A. Las Vegas, Nevada.

Q. "It's Such a Pretty World Today" went number one for what performer in 1967?

A. Wynn Stewart.

Q. What is Eddy Arnold's full name?

A. Richard Edward Arnold.

Q. In what year did Roger Miller have his smash hit "Chug-a-Lug"?

A. 1964.

Q. What performer, born in Robbinsville, North Carolina, was selected by the CMA as Entertainer of the Year in 1977?

A. Ronnie Milsap.

Q. What country artist had three million-seller hits in 1950 with "Chattanooga Shoe Shine Boy," "Steal Away," and "Just a Closer Walk with Thee"?

A. Red Foley.

Q. What instrument did Tennessee Ernie Ford play in his school band?

A. Trombone.

◆

Q. What was George Strait's first Top-10 single after his signing with MCA Records in 1981?

A. "Unwound."

◆

Q. What was Jim Reeves's greatest all-time chartbuster, which was released in 1959?

A. "He'll Have to Go."

◆

Q. What was the actual surname of Marvin Rainwater, who used his mother's maiden name?

A. Percy.

◆

Q. Nat Stuckey had what major hit with RCA in 1968?

A. "Plastic Saddle."

◆

Q. "Looking for Love" from the soundtrack of the movie *Urban Cowboy* was a number-one hit for what country artist?

A. Johnny Lee.

◆

Q. In 1981 what single went Top-10 in the country charts for Jerry Lee Lewis?

A. "Thirty-Nine and Holding."

Hank Williams and his Drifting Cowboys band. Born on September 17, 1923, in the community of Mount Olive, Alabama, Hank Williams grew up in the depression-era poverty of rural America. His childhood became even more tragic with his father's illness, which placed him in the VA hospital by the time Hank was seven years old. Hank learned about music and liquor at an early age and by the early 1940s he was already having serious problems with alcohol, problems that would ultimately take his marriage, his career, and his life. Hank was one of country music's first true superstars, and his legacy of songs, including "I Can't Help It If I'm Still in Love with You," "Cold, Cold Heart," "Your Cheatin' Heart," "Hey, Good-Lookin'," and "I'm So Lonesome I Could Cry" set the standards for pure simplicity and poetry in pop as well as country songwriting. He died on January 1, 1953, at the age of twenty-nine, in the back seat of his powder blue Cadillac convertible, on the way to a New Year's Day concert in Canton, Ohio. [Photo Courtesy of Les Leverett]

Q. What Cape Girardeau, Missouri, native had a major hit in 1974 with "I Can Help"?

A. Billy Swan.

———◆———

Q. What is the stage name of Alabama native Jimmy Loden?

A. Sonny James.

———◆———

Q. Before coming to Nashville in 1972, under what name did Joe Sun (James Paulson) work with several Chicago-area bands?

A. Jack Daniels.

———◆———

Q. Where was Mel Tillis born on August 8, 1932?

A. Tampa, Florida.

———◆———

Q. Sol is the actual first name of what country and western performer, who was born in Ramsey, Illinois?

A. Tex Williams.

———◆———

Q. Who was billed as the High Sheriff?

A. Ford Rush.

———◆———

Q. What was the occupation at age thirteen of Oklahoma-born singer-songwriter Floyd Tillman?

A. Western Union messenger.

Country Music Magazine

Inaugural issue: September 1972
Featured two Johnny Cash articles, one excerpted from a book
    by Christopher Wren, the other by columnist Jack Hurst
Other feature stories: Elvis, Tom T. Hall, Conway Twitty,
    trucking music
Columns: "Down Home and Around" (by Dixie Deen Hall),
    "People on the Scene" (spotlighting new thirteen-year-old
    artist Tanya Tucker), "Gospel Music"
Album reviews: Bill Monroe's *Uncle Pen;* Dave Dudley's *The
    Original Traveling Man; I Saw The Light With Some Help
    From My Friends* by Earl Scruggs; Porter Wagoner's
    Ballads of Love; Freddie Hart's *Bless Your Heart*; *The
    Best of George Jones; Volume I;* and *God Bless America
    Again* by Loretta Lynn
Film reviews: *J. W. Coop* and *The Honkers*
Publisher: John Killion; Editor: Peter McCabe
Single-copy cost: 75¢; yearly subscription: $6.00

Q. Who was Ernest Tubb's first wife, the mother of Justin?

A. Lois Elaine Cook.

◆

Q. Lonnie Donegan had a Top-5 hit in Britain with his version of what 1959 Johnny Horton hit?

A. "Battle of New Orleans."

◆

Q. What country star of the 1970s taught karate at the Los Angeles Police Academy during the 1950s?

A. Freddie Hart.

◆

Q. Who is known as the International Ambassador of Country Music?

A. George Hamilton IV.

Q. Who was born Harold Lloyd Jenkins in Friars Point, Mississippi, on September 1, 1933?

A. Conway Twitty.

———◆———

Q. How many number-one hits did Johnny Rodriguez have in 1975?

A. Three.

———◆———

Q. In 1977 what Kenny Rogers single went number one and was recognized by the CMA as both Song of the Year and Single of the Year?

A. "Lucille."

———◆———

Q. Under what name did T. G. Sheppard record pop-style material on the Atlantic label?

A. Brian Stacy.

———◆———

Q. After leaving Emmylou Harris's band in 1980, Ricky Skaggs recorded what album on the Sugar Hill label?

A. *Sweet Temptation.*

———◆———

Q. Who had Top-10 singles in 1957 with "I Found My Girl in the U.S.A." and "Dark Hollow"?

A. Jimmie Skinner.

———◆———

Q. Lyle Lovett earned a degree with what two majors at Texas A&M?

A. Journalism and German.

Q. Mike Reid's first number-one single, "Walk on Faith," came from what album?

A. *Turning for Home.*

◆

Q. What was the title of Ricky Skaggs's first Nashville album on the Epic label?

A. *Waitin' for the Sun to Shine.*

◆

Q. Little Jimmy Dickens first worked under what stage title?

A. Jimmy the Kid.

◆

Q. Michael Martin Murphey has written pop and country hits for himself and others. Name his two best-known pop hits.

A. "Geronimo's Cadillac" and "Wildfire."

◆

Q. What Oklahoma native, known for such singles as "Till I See You Again" and "Praying for Rain," wrote "Velvet Chains" for Gary Morris?

A. Kevin Welch.

◆

Q. Reprise recording artist Michael White studied for what career while in college?

A. The ministry.

◆

Q. The guitar-shaped swimming pool belonging to what star became a major Nashville tourist attraction?

A. Webb Pierce.

Q. What artist worked on a degree in veterinary medicine at Emory University in Atlanta, Georgia?

A. Roy Drusky.

———◆———

Q. Who became the second wife of Hank Williams Jr. in April 1971?

A. Gwen Yeargain.

———◆———

Q. In 1957 what RCA release provided Jim Reeves with his third million-selling record?

A. "Four Walls."

———◆———

Q. At what age did Bobby Wright become a recording artist with Decca Records?

A. Eleven.

———◆———

Q. He's had only thirteen country hits in twenty-three years but is one of America's most popular touring artists. His fans are known as Parrotheads. Name him.

A. Jimmy Buffett.

———◆———

Q. Name Steve Earle's 1995 Grammy-nominated comeback album.

A. *Train a Comin'*.

———◆———

Q. Collin Raye has had many memorable songs. Name his heart-wrenching 1994 ballad about an alcoholic struggling to remain sober.

A. "Little Rock," written by Tom Douglas.

Q. The career of what western swing star was ended when he was convicted of killing his wife, Ella Mae?

A. Spade Cooley.

———◆———

Q. What Alan Jackson single is a tribute to Hank Williams?

A. "Midnight in Montgomery."

———◆———

Q. Who recorded the album *Too Dumb for New York, Too Ugly for L. A.?*

A. Waylon Jennings.

———◆———

Q. Who soared into country music stardom with the number-one video and Top-5 single "Cadillac Style"?

A. Sammy Kershaw.

———◆———

Q. During the 1980s what recording artist simultaneously had eight albums on *Billboard*'s country charts?

A. Hank Williams Jr.

———◆———

Q. In 1947 what Tex Williams record sold two and one-half million copies?

A. "Smoke! Smoke! Smoke! (That Cigarette)."

———◆———

Q. Who is Dolly Parton's "Romeo" in her 1993 video of the same title?

A. Billy Ray Cyrus.

Q. In 1991 what country music star's sentence for shooting a man in an Ohio bar was commuted by the governor of the state?

A. Johnny PayCheck.

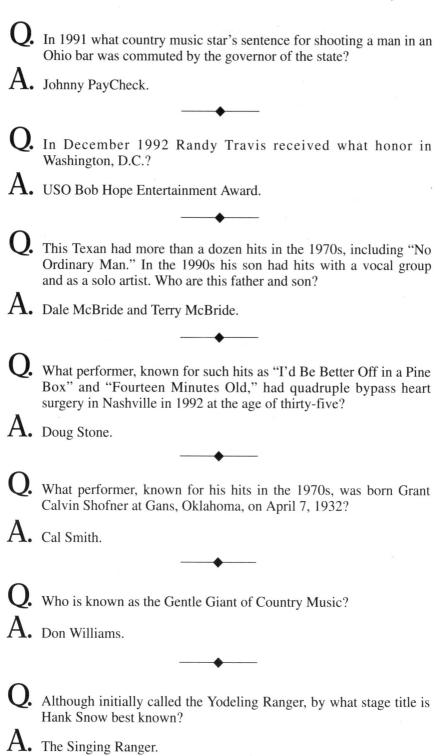

Q. In December 1992 Randy Travis received what honor in Washington, D.C.?

A. USO Bob Hope Entertainment Award.

Q. This Texan had more than a dozen hits in the 1970s, including "No Ordinary Man." In the 1990s his son had hits with a vocal group and as a solo artist. Who are this father and son?

A. Dale McBride and Terry McBride.

Q. What performer, known for such hits as "I'd Be Better Off in a Pine Box" and "Fourteen Minutes Old," had quadruple bypass heart surgery in Nashville in 1992 at the age of thirty-five?

A. Doug Stone.

Q. What performer, known for his hits in the 1970s, was born Grant Calvin Shofner at Gans, Oklahoma, on April 7, 1932?

A. Cal Smith.

Q. Who is known as the Gentle Giant of Country Music?

A. Don Williams.

Q. Although initially called the Yodeling Ranger, by what stage title is Hank Snow best known?

A. The Singing Ranger.

It took David Lee Murphy a number of years and three singles to become an "overnight success" in 1995 with his cowritten ode to the good life, "Party Crowd." That anthemic single and his self-written number-one follow-up, "Dust on the Bottle," propelled his Out with a Bang *album to gold status, setting the stage for his 1996 CD,* Gettin' out the Good Stuff. *Murphy's career is a study in determination and patience: He kept working for years, honing his craft, until MCA's Tony Brown signed him up, first releasing his "Just Once" for the soundtrack album of the rodeo movie* 8 Seconds. [NAOMI KALTMAN PHOTO PROVIDED BY MCA NASHVILLE]

Q. What Texan, born near Houston in 1895, was billed as the Original Singing Cowboy?

A. Carl T. Sprague.

◆

Q. In 1973 what single earned Joe Stampley his first number-one hit?

A. "Soul Song."

◆

Q. Kansan Kenny Starr had what number-two single in 1976?

A. "The Blind Man in the Bleachers."

Q. In 1977 who had hits with "Slide off Your Satin Sheets," "I'm the Only Hell My Mama Ever Raised," and "Take This Job and Shove It"?

A. Johnny PayCheck.

———◆———

Q. What was Hank Penny's longest-running hit on King Records?

A. "My Bloodshot Eyes."

———◆———

Q. What performer's actual name was David Luke Myrick?

A. T. Texas Tyler.

———◆———

Q. What descriptive title was often applied before Jim Reeves's name?

A. Gentleman.

———◆———

Q. Name Tracy Byrd's birthplace and his first chart single.

A. Byrd was born in Vidor, Texas, and in 1992 had a modest hit with "That's the Thing about a Memory."

———◆———

Q. Texas-born Rodney Crowell formed what band at age fifteen and cowrote what hit song with Roy Orbison?

A. Crowell formed the Arbitrators in 1965 and had a number-eleven hit in 1992 with "What Kind of Love."

———◆———

Q. In what area of studies did Leroy Van Dyke receive a degree from the University of Missouri?

A. Agriculture.

Q. What Texan had hits in 1964 with "Circumstances" and "Cross the Brazos at Waco"?

A. Billy Walker.

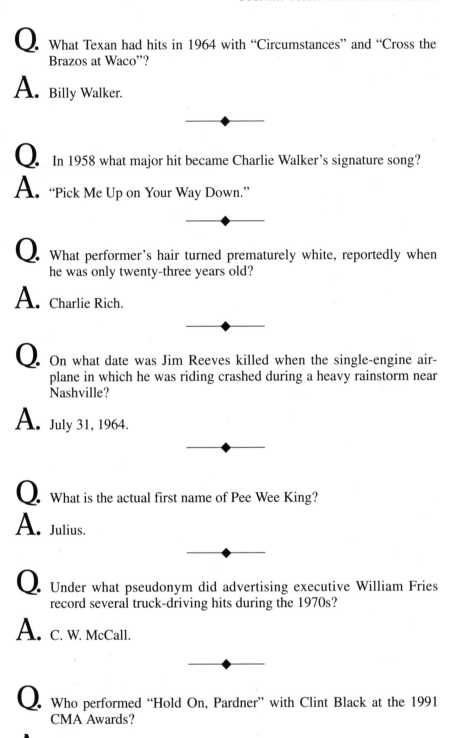

Q. In 1958 what major hit became Charlie Walker's signature song?

A. "Pick Me Up on Your Way Down."

Q. What performer's hair turned prematurely white, reportedly when he was only twenty-three years old?

A. Charlie Rich.

Q. On what date was Jim Reeves killed when the single-engine airplane in which he was riding crashed during a heavy rainstorm near Nashville?

A. July 31, 1964.

Q. What is the actual first name of Pee Wee King?

A. Julius.

Q. Under what pseudonym did advertising executive William Fries record several truck-driving hits during the 1970s?

A. C. W. McCall.

Q. Who performed "Hold On, Pardner" with Clint Black at the 1991 CMA Awards?

A. Roy Rogers.

Country music's best-known announcer-host Ralph Emery and western swing legend Hank Thompson on the set of Nashville Now *in the mid-1980s.* [PHOTO COURTESY OF SKIP JACKSON]

Q. Garth Brooks attended Oklahoma State University on what kind of athletic scholarship?

A. Track and field (he threw the javelin).

Q. What country and western singer, born in Texas on January 12, 1905, appeared in almost eighty films?

A. Tex Ritter.

Q. With what malady was singer-songwriter Red Steagall stricken at age fifteen?

A. Polio.

Q. O. B. McClinton attended what Mississippi school on a choir scholarship?

A. Rust College.

Q. In 1982 what release became Steve Wariner's first number-one single?

A. "All Roads Lead to You."

Q. Joplin, Missouri, native Dennis Weaver recorded his first album on what label in 1972?

A. Impress.

Q. What famed British rocker played guitar and wrote John Anderson's 1992 hit "When It Comes to You"?

A. Mark Knopfler of Dire Straits.

Q. In what year did Freddy Weller have a Top-10 country hit single with "The Games People Play"?

A. 1969.

Q. Billy Edd Wheeler wrote and released what hit in 1964?

A. "Ode to the Little Brown Shack out Back."

Q. In what year did Conway Twitty have his now-classic hit "Hello Darlin'"?

A. 1970.

Q. From what high school in Greenup County, Kentucky, did Billy Ray Cyrus graduate in 1979?

A. Russell High School.

Q. For what company did Joe Diffie work after moving to Nashville in December 1986?

A. Gibson Guitar Company.

Q. What was Marty Robbins's final single to climb into the Top 10?

A. "Honky-Tonk Man" (1983).

Q. Who was the first country singer to perform at the London Palladium?

A. Slim Whitman.

Q. In a 1980 British poll, what Texan was voted Country Artist of the Decade?

A. Don Williams.

Q. Where was Randall Hank Williams (Hank Williams Jr.) born on May 26, 1949?

A. Shreveport, Louisiana.

Q. Who had a mild hit on the Monument label in 1971 with "The Night Miss Nancy Ann's Hotel for Single Girls Burned Down"?

A. Tex Williams.

Q. Who is known as the Sheriff?

A. Faron Young.

Q. How many encores of "Lovesick Blues" did twenty-five-year-old Hank Williams Sr. do at his historic June 11, 1949, appearance on *The Grand Ole Opry*?

A. Six.

Q. What left-handed guitar picker was known as the Talking Blues Man?

A. Robert Lunn.

Q. Stacy Dean Campbell, who has been called the James Dean of country music, was born in what New Mexico town?

A. Carlsbad.

RCA Records released Porter Wagoner's "Company's Coming" on September 3, 1954. It would be a September 11 demo session, however, consisting of forty dollars' worth of studio time at KWTO in Springfield, Missouri, which would produce the biggest hit of Porter's career, "A Satisfied Mind." RCA released the demo cut "as-is" in April 1955, and "A Satisfied Mind" stayed in the Billboard *charts for thirty-three weeks. Porter was born in West Plains, Missouri, on August 12, 1927. His early hits of the 1950s propelled him into a successful career as a performer and music businessman that has spanned several decades.* [PHOTO COURTESY OF PORTER WAGONER ENTERPRISES]

Q. In what Kentucky town were both Dwight Yoakam and Patty Loveless born?

A. Pikeville.

◆

Q. Luther Ossenbrink was known by what stage name on *The National Barn Dance*?

A. Arkie, the Arkansas Woodchopper.

◆

Q. How old was Roy Acuff when he died of congestive heart failure on November 23, 1992?

A. Eighty-nine.

◆

Q. Joe Diffie's first album on the Epic label, *A Thousand Winding Roads,* yielded how many consecutive number-one singles?

A. Four.

◆

Q. What western swing pioneer got his nickname from cards he received in a poker game?

A. Spade Cooley.

◆

Q. Doug Stone's first musical job was playing drums for what band?

A. Country Rhythm Playboys.

◆

Q. What Mississippian began playing mandolin in Lester Flatt's band at age thirteen?

A. Marty Stuart.

Q. What Don Williams recording, which was the B side of a single in the United States, was a Top-10 single in Britain?

A. "I Recall a Gypsy Woman."

———◆———

Q. How old was Hank Williams Sr. when he died?

A. Twenty-nine.

———◆———

Q. What long-time business and career manager of Randy Travis married him in 1991?

A. Lib Hatcher.

———◆———

Q. Which country music performer was asked to leave the premises after refusing to sing a song at a taping for the CMA's thirtieth anniversary celebration in 1993?

A. Ricky Van Shelton.

———◆———

Q. What two country stars have performed "The Star-Spangled Banner" at the Super Bowl?

A. Charley Pride (1974) and Garth Brooks (1993).

———◆———

Q. Who is known as the Man in Black?

A. Johnny Cash.

———◆———

Q. By what nickname is Little Jimmy Dickens known?

A. Tater.

Q. What country star began singing in a children's church choir in his hometown of Marietta, Georgia?

A. Travis Tritt.

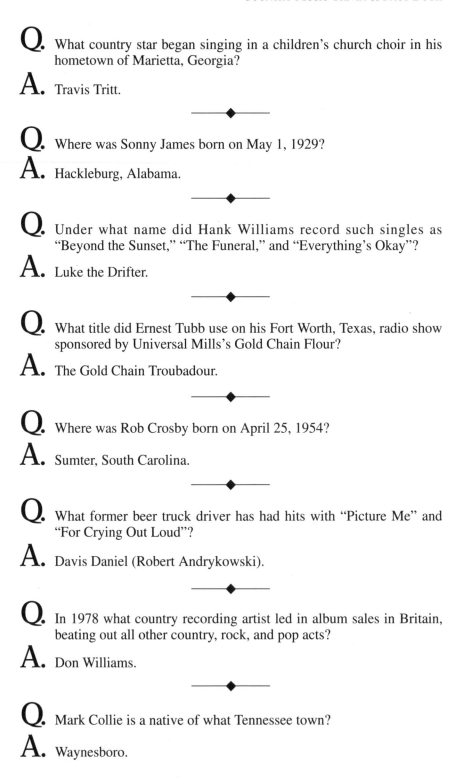

Q. Where was Sonny James born on May 1, 1929?

A. Hackleburg, Alabama.

Q. Under what name did Hank Williams record such singles as "Beyond the Sunset," "The Funeral," and "Everything's Okay"?

A. Luke the Drifter.

Q. What title did Ernest Tubb use on his Fort Worth, Texas, radio show sponsored by Universal Mills's Gold Chain Flour?

A. The Gold Chain Troubadour.

Q. Where was Rob Crosby born on April 25, 1954?

A. Sumter, South Carolina.

Q. What former beer truck driver has had hits with "Picture Me" and "For Crying Out Loud"?

A. Davis Daniel (Robert Andrykowski).

Q. In 1978 what country recording artist led in album sales in Britain, beating out all other country, rock, and pop acts?

A. Don Williams.

Q. Mark Collie is a native of what Tennessee town?

A. Waynesboro.

Q. Hank Snow had what tongue-twisting number-one hit single in 1962?

A. "I've Been Everywhere."

———◆———

Q. Who was known for such truck-driving hits as "Giddyup Go," "Phantom 309," and "Teddy Bear"?

A. Red Sovine.

———◆———

Q. Near what Texas town was Johnny Horton killed in a head-on collision on November 5, 1960?

A. Milano.

———◆———

Q. What was Cal Smith's 1974 hit single that earned him a CMA Single of the Year award?

A. "Country Bumpkin."

———◆———

Q. From 1949 through 1953 Hank Williams had how many Top-10 singles on the *Billboard* charts?

A. Thirty-three.

———◆———

Q. Who recorded under the pseudonym Scotty Wayne?

A. Freddy Fender.

———◆———

Q. What country star at one time recorded under the pseudonym Corky Jones?

A. Buck Owens.

Q. What was Little Jimmy Dickens's 1965 crossover hit?

A. "May the Bird of Paradise Fly up Your Nose."

———◆———

Q. In 1986 what was Randy Travis's first major country music award?

A. ACM Top New Male Vocalist for 1985.

———◆———

Q. What artist, known for such hits as "Love, Me" and "Every Second," was born in DeQueen, Arkansas?

A. Collin Raye (Floyd Collin Wray).

———◆———

Q. What South Carolinian had a number-one hit single with "There Ain't Nothin' Wrong with the Radio"?

A. Aaron Tippin.

———◆———

Q. Who left home at age twelve to join Lester Flatt's band and then linked up with Johnny Cash, Doc Watson, and the Sullivan family before he was twenty-one?

A. Marty Stuart.

———◆———

Q. What former semi-truck driver got his first national attention with "They've Been Talkin' about Me"?

A. Jeff Knight.

———◆———

Q. In 1991 what country superstar turned down a chance to tour with Dire Straits?

A. Vince Gill was offered a role as guitarist and backup singer for a three-year world tour.

Q. At age six what performer sang "San Antonio Rose" with Bob Wills over radio station WBAP in Fort Worth, Texas?

A. Lee Roy Parnell.

———◆———

Q. What Floridian is known for such hits as "Only Here for a Little While" and "Somewhere in My Broken Heart"?

A. Billy Dean.

———◆———

Q. One of Martin Delray's secret dreams is to climb what mountain?

A. Mount Everest.

———◆———

Q. Stanthorpe, Queensland, Australia, is the birthplace of what Liberty recording artist?

A. James Blundell.

———◆———

Q. Where did Marty Brown record his first demos?

A. His bathroom.

———◆———

Q. Neotraditionalist Larry Boone used to play for tips at what Nashville attraction?

A. Country Music Wax Museum.

———◆———

Q. What former musical director for a show on the Nashville Network had a number-one hit single with "Leap of Faith"?

A. Lionel Cartwright.

Q. "Someone Else's Star" paved the way in 1995 for a gold-selling record for what artist?

A. Bryan White.

Q. What was West Virginia native Red Sovine's real name?

A. Woodrow Wilson Sovine.

Q. What is Mercury/Polygram recording artist Jeff Chance's actual last name?

A. Barosh.

Q. Where in Austin, Texas, did Johnny Horton have his last club date before he died in 1960?

A. Skyline Club (also the last club date for Hank Williams).

Q. Who gave Mac Davis the title the Song Painter?

A. Glen Campbell.

Q. What two performers teamed up for the 1991–92 No Hats Tour, then reunited to tour again in 1996 as Double Trouble?

A. Marty Stuart and Travis Tritt.

Q. What Florida-born singer-songwriter had a hit single in 1979 with "Coca-Cola Cowboy"?

A. Mel Tillis.

Q. Although he claimed to be from Oklahoma, where was Lloyd "Cowboy" Copas actually born?

A. Blue Creek, Ohio.

Q. What singing cowboy started his music career by singing at the Indian Creek Baptist Church in Tioga, Texas, where his grandfather was the pastor?

A. Gene Autry.

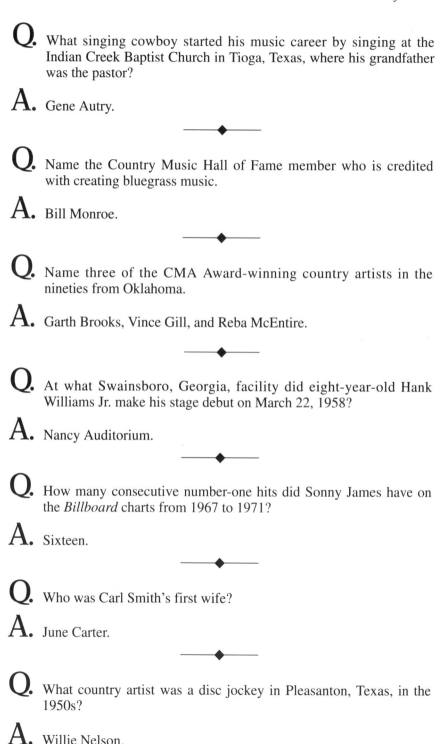

Q. Name the Country Music Hall of Fame member who is credited with creating bluegrass music.

A. Bill Monroe.

Q. Name three of the CMA Award-winning country artists in the nineties from Oklahoma.

A. Garth Brooks, Vince Gill, and Reba McEntire.

Q. At what Swainsboro, Georgia, facility did eight-year-old Hank Williams Jr. make his stage debut on March 22, 1958?

A. Nancy Auditorium.

Q. How many consecutive number-one hits did Sonny James have on the *Billboard* charts from 1967 to 1971?

A. Sixteen.

Q. Who was Carl Smith's first wife?

A. June Carter.

Q. What country artist was a disc jockey in Pleasanton, Texas, in the 1950s?

A. Willie Nelson.

Q. In 1983 Kix Brooks and Ronnie Dunn each had hit singles as solo artists. What were those two minor chart hits?

A. Brooks—"Baby, When Your Heart Breaks Down." Dunn—"It's Written All over Your Face."

Q. How many copies did Garth Brooks's second album, *No Fences,* sell during its first ten days in the stores?

A. Seven hundred thousand.

Q. What is Johnny Rodriguez's full name?

A. Juan Raul Davis Rodriguez.

Q. On what date did Marty Robbins become a *Grand Ole Opry* member?

A. January 19, 1953.

Q. Who introduced Elvis at his October 2, 1954, appearance on *The Grand Ole Opry?*

A. Hank Snow.

Q. Although raised in Texas, Clint Black was born in what state?

A. New Jersey.

Q. What was the last song recorded by Jimmie Rodgers in New York on May 24, 1933, just two days before his death from tuberculosis?

A. "Years Ago."

Dwight Yoakam, one of modern country music's most uncompromising new traditionalists, has helped bring the term hillbilly *back into respectability and fashion. Born in the same southeastern Kentucky, Appalachian coal region as Loretta Lynn, Yoakam was raised in Columbus, Ohio, where his family's country ways were treated with the same kind of derision that the "Okies" had received in California a generation earlier. He was performing throughout the Ohio Valley by the time he finished high school and moved to the Los Angeles area in the early 1980s. He played the southern California honky-tonks, dubbed the "cowpunk" circuit, where he met guitarist Pete Anderson. Soon after Anderson joined his band, they began producing records. His first number-one chart hit, "The Streets of Bakersfield," was a duet with his idol, Buck Owens. Yoakam eventually cut three top-selling albums before taking a rest from touring. His latest album,* Gone, *was released in late 1995.* [PHOTO COURTESY OF ALAN MAYOR]

Q. Name George Strait's biggest-selling album as of 1996, with five million copies.

A. *Pure Country.*

Q. Who won the 1990 Marlboro Talent Search?

A. Ronnie Dunn.

Q. What retail position is the only nonmusical job Mark Chesnutt has had?

A. Lawn and garden department sales for Montgomery Ward.

Q. What second album by Alan Jackson, released on the Arista label in May 1991, went platinum?

A. *Don't Rock the Jukebox.*

Q. According to *Radio & Records* magazine, what Hal Ketchum single was the top country radio hit in 1991?

A. "Small Town Saturday Night."

Q. What quirky and talented performer became known for his trademark "tall" hair?

A. Lyle Lovett.

Q. What performer, whose actual name is Doug Brooks, got his stage name from a song he wrote?

A. Doug Stone, from "Heart of Stone."

Oklahoma-born Toby Keith was discovered by Harold Shedd, the label executive who also produced Alabama and K. T. Oslin. Keith was an oil field worker and a semipro football player before getting his record deal with Mercury in 1993. His first single, "Should've Been a Cowboy," rocketed to number one and also made the pop Top 100. More hits, including "He Ain't Worth Missing" and "A Little Less Talk and a Lot More Action," followed. Mercury reactivated the Polydor label in 1994 with Keith becoming their flagship artist. Another corporate move in 1996 found Keith moving to A&M Records' new Nashville operation with his "Does That Blue Moon Ever Shine on You" becoming the label's first release. [Mark Tucker Photo Provided by A&M Records]

Q. What's the biggest-selling country album of all time, as of 1996?

A. Garth Brooks's *No Fences* has been certified for fourteen million, followed by his own *Ropin' the Wind*, certified for twelve million.

———◆———

Q. What is the actual surname of Randy Travis, who was born in Marshville, North Carolina, on May 4, 1959?

A. Traywick.

———◆———

Q. In 1990 Mary Jane Thomas became the fourth wife of what star?

A. Hank Williams Jr.

Q. Name the pop megastar who released an album entitled *Tennessee Moon* in 1996.

A. Neil Diamond.

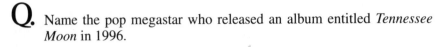

Q. What is tattooed on Aaron Tippin's right biceps?

A. A palmetto tree.

Q. *Life's a Dance* is the title of what Kentucky native's debut single and compact disc?

A. John Michael Montgomery.

Q. What country legends have Music Row side streets named after them?

A. Chet Atkins and Roy Acuff.

FEMALE PERFORMERS

Q. What do the initials in K. T. Oslin's name stand for?

A. Kay Toinette.

—◆—

Q. Paulette Carlson left what group in 1990 to pursue a solo career?

A. Highway 101.

—◆—

Q. In whose honor did the Mississippi state legislature rename a thirteen-mile section of Mississippi Highway 23 in Itawamba County in 1992?

A. Tammy Wynette.

—◆—

Q. In the Ojibwa dialect, what is the meaning of Shania Twain's first name?

A. "I'm on my way."

—◆—

Q. What singer has had the most country hits for an Australian?

A. Diana Trask posted eighteen hits between 1968 and 1981, three more than the better-known Olivia Newton-John.

Q. Who gave Dolly Parton a custom-made Cadillac Eldorado as a Christmas present in 1972?

A. Porter Wagoner.

◆

Q. As a small child what performer lost the pinky finger on her left hand in an accident?

A. Lari White.

◆

Q. On what album did Suzy Bogguss team up with super-picker Chet Atkins?

A. *Simpatico*.

◆

Q. In January 1983 what single became Reba McEntire's first number-one hit?

A. "Can't Even Get the Blues."

◆

Q. What thirteen-year-old received a standing ovation following her rendition of "Paper Roses" at her 1973 *Grand Ole Opry* debut?

A. Lorrie Morgan.

◆

Q. What country star and her producer married in 1989 but kept it a secret for eighteen months?

A. Patty Loveless and Emory Gordy Jr.

◆

Q. Linda Davis is a native of what East Texas town?

A. Gary.

"Little Miss Dynamite," Brenda Lee, in 1959 with her manager (seated) and Nashville recording pioneer Owen Bradley. [PHOTO COURTESY OF CHUCK POWELL]

Q. Whom did Loretta Lynn marry just before her fourteenth birthday?

A. Oliver "Mooney" Lynn.

Q. What singing cowgirl was New York's first hillbilly disc jockey?

A. Rosalie Allen.

Q. What country recording star published a book of "strange" short stories in 1996?

A. CMA Award-winning writer-performer Rosanne Cash issued *Bodies of Water.*

Q. Who was Mindy McCready's first housemate in Nashville?

A. Lukie, her miniature dachshund.

Q. Whom did Reba McEntire marry in 1989?

A. Her manager, Narvel Blackstock.

Q. What country performer's stage name was inspired by the name of a fast-food chain?

A. Crystal Gayle (for Krystal hamburgers).

Q. What Kansas community is Martina McBride's hometown?

A. Sharon.

Q. To whom was Lorrie Morgan married from November 1986 until his untimely death on May 9, 1989?

A. Keith Whitley.

Q. Although she was raised in Mobile, Alabama, and Houston, Texas, K. T. Oslin was born in what Arkansas town?

A. Crossett.

Q. Pam Tillis married what songwriter on Valentine's Day 1991?

A. Bob DiPiero.

Q. Name the female country superstar writer of such songs as "Independence Day" and "You Don't Even Know My Name" who grew up in Colorado after being born in Bronxville, New York.

A. Gretchen Peters.

Q. Who had such hit records as "Baby, Don't Touch Me," "Misty Blue," and "Tear Time"?

A. Wilma Burgess.

———————◆———————

Q. How old was Tanya Tucker when forty-four-year-old Glen Campbell gave her an engagement ring?

A. Twenty-two.

———————◆———————

Q. What female country singer was at one time married to British rocker Nick Lowe?

A. Carlene Carter.

———————◆———————

Q. Which artist's father was an editor for *Life* magazine?

A. Mary Chapin Carpenter.

———————◆———————

Q. What was Patsy Cline's name at birth?

A. Virginia Patterson Hensley.

———————◆———————

Q. Trisha Yearwood was married to what song plugger at EMI Music?

A. Chris Latham.

———————◆———————

Q. What was Sylvia's first release following her signing with RCA in 1979?

A. "You Don't Miss a Thing."

Grammy Awards
Best Country Performance, Female

1964 Dottie West, "Here Comes My Baby"
1965 Jody Miller, "Queen of the House"
1966 Jeannie Seely, "Don't Touch Me"
1967 Tammy Wynette, "I Don't Want to Play House"
1968 Jeannie C. Riley, "Harper Valley P.T.A."
1969 Tammy Wynette, *Stand By Your Man* (Album)
1970 Lynn Anderson, "Rose Garden"
1971 Sammi Smith, "Help Me Make It through the Night"
1972 Donna Fargo, "Happiest Girl in the Whole U.S.A."
1973 Olivia Newton-John, "Let Me Be There"
1974 Anne Murray, *Love Song* (Album)
1975 Linda Ronstadt, "I Can't Help It If I'm Still in Love with You"
1976 Emmylou Harris, *Elite Hotel* (Album)
1977 Crystal Gayle, "Don't It Make My Brown Eyes Blue"
1978 Dolly Parton, *Here You Come Again* (Album)
1979 Emmylou Harris, *Blue Kentucky Girl* (Album)
1980 Anne Murray, "Could I Have This Dance?"
1981 Dolly Parton, "9 to 5"
1982 Juice Newton, "Break It to Me Gently"
1983 Anne Murray, "A Little Good News"
1984 Emmylou Harris, "In My Dreams"
1985 Rosanne Cash, "I Don't Know Why You Don't Want Me"
1986 Reba McEntire, "Whoever's in New England"
1987 K. T. Oslin, "80's Ladies"
1988 K. T. Oslin, "Hold Me"
1989 k. d. lang, *Absolute Torch and Twang* (Album)
1990 Kathy Mattea, "Where've You Been"
1991 Mary Chapin Carpenter, "Down at the Twist and Shout"
1992 Mary Chapin Carpenter, "I Feel Lucky"
1993 Mary Chapin Carpenter, "Passionate Kisses"
1994 Mary Chapin Carpenter, "Shut Up and Kiss Me"
1995 Alison Krauss, "Baby, Now That I've Found You"

Q. Who was Sue Thompson's husband before her marriage to Hank Penny?

A. Dude Martin.

Q. During 1978–79 Kathy Mattea's first job in Nashville was as a tour guide at what attraction?

A. Country Music Hall of Fame and Museum.

Q. In 1952 what female country artist was the first to be charted with a number-one solo single, "It Wasn't God Who Made Honky-Tonk Angels"?

A. Kitty Wells.

Q. In 1964 what self-penned RCA release became Dottie West's first major hit?

A. "Here Comes My Baby."

Q. Who sang the harmony vocals with Martina McBride on her 1993 single "Cheap Whiskey"?

A. Garth Brooks.

Q. Patsy Cline performed what song to win on *The Arthur Godfrey Talent Scout* show in 1957?

A. "Walking after Midnight."

Q. To whom was Jessi Colter married during the late 1950s and early 1960s?

A. Duane Eddy.

Q. What was six-times-married Gus Hardin's birth name?

A. Carolyn Ann Blankenship.

Q. What artist got her stage name because she wore a rattlesnake rattle as an earring?

A. Rattlesnake Annie.

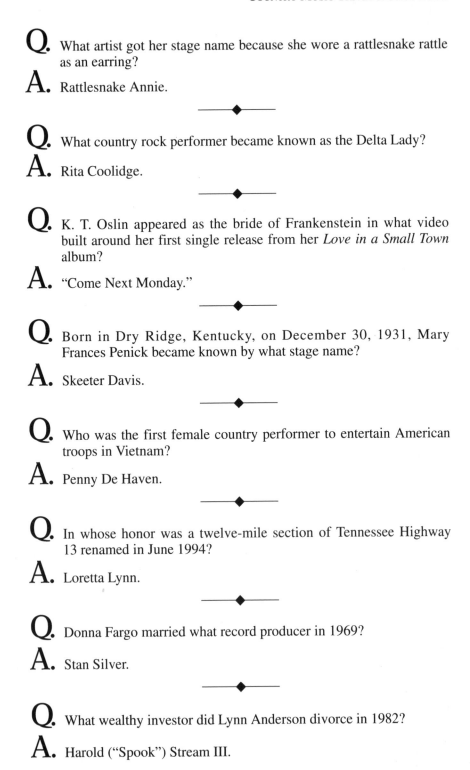

Q. What country rock performer became known as the Delta Lady?

A. Rita Coolidge.

Q. K. T. Oslin appeared as the bride of Frankenstein in what video built around her first single release from her *Love in a Small Town* album?

A. "Come Next Monday."

Q. Born in Dry Ridge, Kentucky, on December 30, 1931, Mary Frances Penick became known by what stage name?

A. Skeeter Davis.

Q. Who was the first female country performer to entertain American troops in Vietnam?

A. Penny De Haven.

Q. In whose honor was a twelve-mile section of Tennessee Highway 13 renamed in June 1994?

A. Loretta Lynn.

Q. Donna Fargo married what record producer in 1969?

A. Stan Silver.

Q. What wealthy investor did Lynn Anderson divorce in 1982?

A. Harold ("Spook") Stream III.

Q. What 1991 Holly Dunn single drew objections from some women listeners?

A. "Maybe I Mean Yes."

◆

Q. What is Donna Fargo's actual name?

A. Yvonne Vaughn.

◆

Q. What longtime *Grand Ole Opry* star was the sister of Tex Owens?

A. Texas Ruby.

◆

Q. What was Chely Wright's first job in Nashville?

A. She sold athletic wear.

◆

Q. Who produced Janie Fricke's first Columbia Records album?

A. Billy Sherrill.

◆

Q. Born Brenda Gail Webb, who is Loretta Lynn's youngest sister?

A. Crystal Gayle.

◆

Q. By what professional name is Mississippi-born Roberta Streeter known?

A. Bobbie Gentry.

◆

Q. What female country star worked in the woods as a foreman on a reforestation crew?

A. Shania Twain.

Q. "Help Me Make It through the Night" on the Mega label became a certified gold hit for what artist in 1971?

A. Sammi Smith.

———◆———

Q. Before she became a Mercury recording star, Terri Clark put on shows at Tootsie's Orchid Lounge that were in what way unusual?

A. Fearing theft, she kept her guitar tied to her wrist while she was offstage.

———◆———

Q. Released on the Capitol label in 1968, what single became Billie Jo Spear's first hit?

A. "He's Got More Love in His Little Finger."

———◆———

Q. What is Bobbie Cryner's favorite hobby?

A. She designs and sews her own stage clothes.

———◆———

Q. Who was recognized by the ACM in 1985 as the 1984 Top New Female Vocalist?

A. Nicolette Larson.

———◆———

Q. Pop crooner k. d. lang was a huge fan of what Country Music Hall of Fame singer, whose last name she incorporated into the name of her own group?

A. Patsy Cline (lang named her band the Reclines).

Canadian-born Shania Twain was the country music success story of 1995 when her second album, The Woman in Me, *racked up sales of five million in its first year of release, the most ever for a new artist. After her first album, filled with the material of other writers, failed to do well, Twain eschewed the Nashville system, married rock producer "Mutt" Lange, and with him cowrote* The Woman in Me, *winning a Grammy for Best Country Album. Twain opted not to give live performances during all of 1995 and into 1996, instead taking shopping center "Fan Appreciation" dates and appearing on carefully chosen and very high-profile awards shows.* [Photo Provided by Mercury Records]

Q. Bobbie Gentry majored in what subject at the University of California at Los Angeles?

A. Philosophy.

◆

Q. What was the amount on the price tag on the late Minnie Pearl's flower-bedecked straw hat?

A. $1.98.

◆

Q. What female country artist was allowed to fly with the U.S. Air Force's Thunderbirds?

A. Barbara Mandrell.

◆

Q. LaCosta is the oldest sister of what other country artist?

A. Tanya Tucker.

◆

Q. With what single did Wanda Jackson have a major hit in Japan during the late 1950s?

A. "Fujiyama Mama."

◆

Q. What 1970 release on the Capitol label was a huge hit on both the country and pop charts for Anne Murray?

A. "Snowbird."

◆

Q. What daughter of Tex Owens was Bob Wills's first female singer?

A. Laura Lee McBride.

Kathy Mattea, who was born in Cross Lanes, West Virginia, in 1959, had her first Top-10 single in 1986 with "Love at the Five and Dime." A string of number-one hits, including "Goin' Gone" and "Eighteen Wheels and a Dozen Roses," led the CMA to recognize Kathy as Vocalist of the Year in both 1989 and 1990. [BY PERMISSION OF MERCURY/POLYGRAM RECORDS]

Q. What's unusual about Grammy winner and accomplished equestrienne Lynn Anderson's performances at rodeos?

A. She sings some songs on horseback (including, at times, the national anthem).

———◆———

Q. What was Molly O'Day's first stage name?

A. Mountain Fern.

———◆———

Q. Name Pam Tillis's first album, released by Warner Brothers in 1983.

A. *Above and Beyond the Doll of Cutey.*

———◆———

Q. What memorial compact disc did Reba McEntire record in honor of her band members killed in a 1991 airplane crash?

A. *For My Broken Heart.*

Radio Barn Dance Shows

The hillbilly radio barn dance name and format were first introduced as early as 1923. The original appearance was probably over WBAP radio in Fort Worth, Texas, when old-time fiddler and Confederate veteran Capt. M. J. Bonner's string band played one and one-half hours of square-dance music to a huge audience response.

The following list is far from comprehensive; it does, however, include a sampling of the most prominent barn dances across the country from the 1920s through the dawn of the television era in the mid-twentieth century. The lists of cast members are also intended to be symbolic rather than complete. An entire book would be necessary to adequately detail all the radio barn dance shows, their histories, and personnel.

———————◆———————

■ *Big D Jamboree* (KRLD, Dallas, Texas). *First show:* 1947. *Broadcast from:* Sportatorium. *Other names: Lone Star Barn Dance. Cast members:* Hilltop Ramblers, Morris Brothers, Okie Jones, Otis West, the Callahans, Buddy Griffin (brother of Rex), Al Turner, Gene O'Quinn, Sonny James, Ray Price, Floyd Tillman, Al Dexter, Slim Whitman, Bill Walker (the Travelin' Texan).

■ *Boone County Jamboree* (WLW, Cincinnati, Ohio). *First show:* 1938. *Other names: Midwestern Hayride. TV info:* WLW-TV; local broadcasts began in 1948; summer replacement show for NBC and ABC during 1950s; syndicated in 1960s. *Cast members:* Hugh Cross, Shug Fisher, Lulu Belle and Scotty.

■ *Crazy Barn Dance* (WBT, Charlotte, North Carolina). *First show:* 1933. *Miscellaneous facts:* Show sponsored by the Crazy Water Crystals Company of Mineral Wells, Texas. (Sold white concentrate of minerals taken from the Crazy Well in Mineral Wells as laxative.) Many bands used the word *crazy* in name. *Cast members:* J. E. Mainer and the Crazy Mountaineers, Dick Hartman's Crazy Tennessee Ramblers, Dixon Brothers, Fisher Hendley, Charles Hunter, Bob Phillips, Carolina Vagabonds, Fred Kirby (the Crazy Cavalier), M. P. Medford, Songfellows.

■ *Grand Ole Opry* (WSM, Nashville, Tennessee). *First show:* November 28, 1925 (named *Grand Ole Opry* on

(continued next page)

December 10, 1927). *Broadcast from:* National Life Building, Hillsboro Theatre, Dixie Tabernacle, War Memorial Building, Ryman Auditorium, and Grand Ole Opry House. *Miscellaneous facts:* Called *WSM Barn Dance* until George D. Hay renamed it *The Grand Ole Opry* in 1927; WSM call letters stand for We Shield Millions, a motto of the National Life and Accident Insurance Company, owners of the radio station; Uncle Jimmy Thompson and his niece, Eva Thompson Jones, were the first performers on the *WSM Barn Dance*; one of the only barn dance shows still in existence today. Cast members (partial listing): DeFord Bailey, Uncle Dave Macon, Roy Acuff, Fruit Jar Drinkers, Dr. Humphrey Bate and the Possum Hunters, the Gully Jumpers, the Crook Brothers, Kirk and Sam McGee, Hank Williams Sr., Hank Snow, Eddy Arnold, Minnie Pearl, Patsy Cline, Little Jimmy Dickens, Porter Wagoner, Bill Monroe, Jim Reeves, Jean Shepard, Carl Smith, Ernest Tubb, Del Wood, Faron Young, Wilma Lee and Stoney Cooper, Don Gibson, Hawkshaw Hawkins, Grandpa Jones, George Jones, Loretta Lynn, Tammy Wynette, Rod Brasfield, Whitey Ford (the Duke of Paducah), George Hamilton IV, Red Foley, Johnny and Jack, Kitty Wells, Webb Pierce, Red Sovine, Archie Campbell, the Carter Family, Cowboy Copas, Flatt and Scruggs, Ferlin Husky, Stonewall Jackson, Stringbean, George Morgan, Moon Mullican, the Louvin Brothers, Jim and Jesse, Reba McEntire, Emmylou Harris, Marty Stuart, Alan Jackson, Travis Tritt, Randy Travis, Ricky Skaggs, Vince Gill, Garth Brooks. The complete roster reads like a "Who's Who" of country music, past and present.

■ *Iowa Barn Dance Frolic* (WHO, Des Moines). *First show:* late 1920s. *Broadcast from:* the mythical town of Sunset Corners at the Shrine Auditorium. *Miscellaneous facts:* Eclectic mixture of old-fashioned pop music, barbershop singing, novelty tunes, folk music. *Cast members:* Texas Ruby, Zeke Clements, Lem and Martha, Tillie and the Sheriff, Al Clauser and his Oklahoma Outlaws, Callico Maids, Pals of the Prairie, Barnyard Pete, Smilin' Sam, Buddy Webster and his Borderland Buckaroos, Jerry and Zelda, the D Sisters.

■ *Louisiana Hayride* (KWKH, Shreveport). *First show:* April 3, 1948. *Broadcast from:* Shreveport Municipal Auditorium. *Miscellaneous facts: Saturday Night Round-Up* had been broadcast over KWKH prior to WW II, then had closed during the war years. *Cast members:* Hank Williams

(continued next page)

Sr., Johnny and Jack, Kitty Wells, Bailes Brothers, the Browns, Zeke Clements, Red Sovine, Billy Walker, Slim Whitman, Faron Young, Tillman Franks, Goldie Hill, Tommy Hill, Merle Kilgore, Hank Locklin, Elvis Presley, Jim Reeves, Don Warden, Webb Pierce, Johnny Horton, Bill Carlisle, Maddox Brothers and Rose.

■ *Mid-Day Merry-Go-Round* (WNOX, Knoxville, Tennessee). *First show:* 1936. *Broadcast from:* WNOX, Market Hall, Old Lyric Theatre. *Other names: WNOX Carnival, Tennessee Barn Dance* (Saturday night program only). *Cast members:* Archie Campbell, Buckeye Buckaroos, the Tropical Islanders, Lost John Miller, Guy Campbell, Arthur Q. Smith, Bill Carlisle, Cliff Carlisle, Chet Atkins, Don Gibson, the Carter Family, Homer and Jethro, Johnny and Jack, Kitty Wells, Eddie Hill.

■ *National Barn Dance* (WLS, Chicago, Illinois). *First show:* April 19, 1924. *Broadcast from:* Sherman Hotel, Eighth Street Theatre. *Miscellaneous facts:* WLS (World's Largest Store) founded by Sears, Roebuck and Company; the nation's leading country music show until superseded by *The Grand Ole Opry*; first regularly broadcast country music jamboree. *Cast members:* Bradley Kincaid, Gene Autry, Arkie the Arkansas Woodchopper, Prairie Ramblers, Patsy Montana, Jenny Lou Carson, Pat Buttram, Eddie Dean, Mac and Bob, Karl and Harty, Linda Parker, John Lair's Cumberland Ridge Runners (first called Renfro Valley Boys), Doc Hopkins, Red Foley, Coon Creek Girls, Lulu Belle and Scotty, Rex Allen, Homer and Jethro, Bob Atcher, Johnny Bond, Gene and Glenn, George Gobel, Girls of the Golden West (Millie and Dolly Good), Gene Ruppe, Clayton McMichen, Hoosier Hot Shots.

■ *Old Dominion Barn Dance* (WRVA, Richmond, Virginia). *First show:* early 1940s. *Broadcast from:* WRVA Theatre. *Miscellaneous facts:* Sunshine Sue (Sue Workman) presided over *The Old Dominion Barn Dance* from 1946 to 1957. *Other names: New Dominion Barn Dance. Cast members:* Reno and Smiley, Mack Magaha, Joe and Rose Lee Maphis, Barbara Allen, Bobby Atkins, Grandpa Jones, Virginia Mountain Boys, Chief Powhatan, Mac Wiseman, Brennan Twins, Jim Eanes, Knight Sisters, Janis Martin.

■ *Renfro Valley Barn Dance* (Renfro Valley, Kentucky). *First show:* November 4, 1939 (first broadcast over WLW, Cincinnati, in 1937 and from Dayton, Ohio, in 1938).

(continued next page)

Miscellaneous facts: Began by folk music collector and authority John Lair, with partners Red and Cotton Foley and Whitey Ford (the Duke of Paducah); offshoot of *WLS National Barn Dance* in Chicago; one of the only barn dance shows still in existence today. *Cast members:* Girls of the Golden West (Millie and Dolly Good), Lulu Belle and Scotty, the Coon Creek Girls, Aunt Idy and Uncle Juney, Slim Miller, Jerry Byrd, Martha Carson, Bess Farmer and the Farmer Sisters, Fairly Holden, Linda Lou Martin, Old Joe Clark, Gabe Tucker.

■ *Wheeling Jamboree* (WWVA, Wheeling, West Virginia). *First show:* January 7, 1933. *Broadcast from:* WWVA studio, Capitol Theatre, Victoria Theatre, Market Auditorium, Virginia Theatre. *Miscellaneous facts:* Discontinued during World War II years; resumed July 13, 1946. *Other names: Jamboree, U.S.A. Cast members:* Harry McAuliffe (Big Slim, the Lone Cowboy), Reno and Smiley, Georgie-Porgie Gang, Doc and Chickie Williams and the Border Riders, Grandpa Jones, Crazy Elmer, Jimmy Martin, Merle Kilgore, Kenny Roberts, Louvin Brothers, Sonny James, Pete Cassell, Lew Childre, Hawkshaw Hawkins, Lone Pine and Betty Cody, Wilma Lee and Stoney Cooper and the Clinch Mountain Clan, George Morgan.

Q. What do Michelle Wright, Lisa Brokop, Terri Clark, and Patricia Conroy have in common?

A. All hail from Canada.

◆

Q. In 1992 who donated five hundred thousand dollars to her native Sevier County, Tennessee, to improve public education?

A. Dolly Parton.

◆

Q. What single on the Challenge label won Jan Howard several awards in 1960?

A. "The One You Slip Around With."

Q. Who took the charts by storm in 1968 with such singles as "D-I-V-O-R-C-E" and "Stand By Your Man"?

A. Tammy Wynette.

Q. What Bridgewater, Nova Scotia, native has been known as Canada's Queen of Country Music?

A. Carroll Baker.

Q. "Somebody's Knockin'" was a Top-10 hit single for what Georgian in 1980?

A. Terri Gibbs.

Q. Shelby Lynne notched her first chart record with what legendary singer?

A. She enjoyed a number-forty-three hit, "If I Could Bottle This Up," with George Jones.

Q. Star, Mississippi, is the hometown of what female country music artist?

A. Faith Hill.

Q. What performer studied drama at Vanderbilt University in Nashville and at the Lee Strasberg Institute in Los Angeles?

A. Rosanne Cash.

Q. Emmylou Harris married what British-born songwriter in 1985?

A. Paul Kennerley.

Born in Seminole, Texas, on October 10, 1958, Tanya Denise Tucker was cutting her first demo record in Las Vegas by age nine. Tanya's 1972 Top-10 single "Delta Dawn" launched her on a run of hits including "Jamestown Ferry," "Blood Red and Goin' Down," and "What's Your Mama's Name?" Throughout her career Tanya has continued to be a hit-maker. [BY PERMISSION OF CAPITOL/NASHVILLE RECORDS.]

Q. What female performer does Trisha Yearwood call her "megahero"?

A. Linda Ronstadt.

———◆———

Q. Whom did George Jones dub the Princess of Country Music?

A. Charly McClain.

———◆———

Q. Besides Loretta, name six country chart artists who have had the last name of Lynn.

A. Jenny Lynn, Judy Lynn, Marcia Lynn, Michelle Lynn, Rebecca Lynn, and Trisha Lynn.

———◆———

Q. Kitty Wells derived her stage name from what source?

A. A folk song, "Sweet Kitty Wells."

Q. Whom did Louise Mandrell marry in 1979?

A. R. C. Bannon (Dan H. Shipley).

Q. Who became known as Little Miss Dynamite?

A. Brenda Lee.

Q. First known as a steel guitar whiz, who has been chosen Best Female Vocalist at the British Country Music Awards more than anyone else in the 1990s?

A. Sarah Jory.

Q. At what age did LaCosta enter her first talent contest, in Snyder, Texas?

A. Four.

Q. What female country performer sang harmony on Ringo Starr's album *Beaucoup of Blues*?

A. Jeannie Kendall.

Q. What country performer was at one time a secretary for the Fifth Dimension?

A. Naomi Judd.

Q. Who was born Rubye Blevins in Hot Springs, Arkansas, on October 30, 1914?

A. Patsy Montana.

Q. At what preparatory school for young women in Nashville did Minnie Pearl receive her education?

A. Ward-Belmont.

◆

Q. What Canadian city is Shania Twain's hometown?

A. Timmins, Ontario.

◆

Q. What was Martina McBride's maiden name?

A. Martina Schiff.

◆

Q. What singer did Dolly Parton replace on Porter Wagoner's television show in 1967?

A. Norma Jean.

CMA Female Vocalist of the Year

1967	Loretta Lynn	1982	Janie Fricke
1968	Tammy Wynette	1983	Janie Fricke
1969	Tammy Wynette	1984	Reba McEntire
1970	Tammy Wynette	1985	Reba McEntire
1971	Lynn Anderson	1986	Reba McEntire
1972	Loretta Lynn	1987	Reba McEntire
1973	Loretta Lynn	1988	K. T. Oslin
1974	Olivia Newton-John	1989	Kathy Mattea
1975	Dolly Parton	1990	Kathy Mattea
1976	Dolly Parton	1991	Tanya Tucker
1977	Crystal Gayle	1992	Mary Chapin Carpenter
1978	Crystal Gayle	1993	Mary Chapin Carpenter
1979	Barbara Mandrell	1994	Pam Tillis
1980	Emmylou Harris	1995	Alison Krauss
1981	Barbara Mandrell		

Q. What British-born, Australia-raised recording artist received the 1974 CMA Female Vocalist of the Year award?

A. Olivia Newton-John.

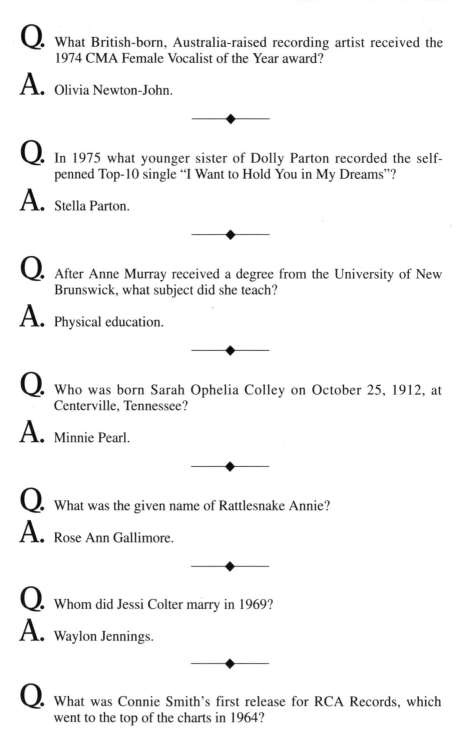

Q. In 1975 what younger sister of Dolly Parton recorded the self-penned Top-10 single "I Want to Hold You in My Dreams"?

A. Stella Parton.

Q. After Anne Murray received a degree from the University of New Brunswick, what subject did she teach?

A. Physical education.

Q. Who was born Sarah Ophelia Colley on October 25, 1912, at Centerville, Tennessee?

A. Minnie Pearl.

Q. What was the given name of Rattlesnake Annie?

A. Rose Ann Gallimore.

Q. Whom did Jessi Colter marry in 1969?

A. Waylon Jennings.

Q. What was Connie Smith's first release for RCA Records, which went to the top of the charts in 1964?

A. "Once a Day."

Q. What 1973 single by Jeanne Pruett became a number-one country hit and number twenty-eight on the pop charts?

A. "Satin Sheets."

Q. What is Lorrie Morgan's full name?

A. Loretta Lynn Morgan.

Q. For what year did Jeannie C. Riley receive a Grammy as Best Country Vocal Performance Female?

A. 1968.

Q. Where was Sylvia born in 1956?

A. Kokomo, Indiana.

Q. How many CMA Awards did Alison Krauss take home from the 1995 ceremony?

A. Four. Krauss won for Best Single, Female Vocalist, the Horizon Award, and Best Vocal Collaboration (with Shenandoah).

Q. After moving to Nashville in the late 1960s, what was the first hit on Dial Records for Australian Diana Trask?

A. "Lock, Stock, and Teardrops."

Q. What female country performer appeared on the cover of *Rolling Stone* magazine as a young teenager?

A. Tanya Tucker.

Q. Whom did Rita Coolidge marry in 1973?

A. Kris Kristofferson.

Q. In what two years was Dolly Parton recognized by the CMA as Female Vocalist of the Year?

A. 1975 and 1976.

Q. Who won a Grammy for Best Female Country and Western Vocal Performance with her 1966 recording of Hank Cochran's composition "Don't Touch Me"?

A. Jeannie Seely.

Q. Trisha Yearwood graduated from what Nashville college with a degree in business administration?

A. Belmont University.

Q. At age fifteen Leona Williams had her own radio show, *Leona Sings*, in what Missouri town?

A. Jefferson City.

Q. What Grammy-winning album, recorded in New Orleans with pop producer Daniel Lanois, did Emmylou Harris refer to as her "strange" album?

A. *Wrecking Ball.*

Q. Whom did Shelly West divorce in 1985?

A. Allen Frizzell.

Q. For what did Shania Twain win a Grammy Award in 1996?

A. Country Album of the Year for *The Woman in Me.*

Q. In 1985 while Rhonda Vincent was on leave of absence from her family's bluegrass group and working with Jim Ed Brown's band, her father hired what twelve-year-old replacement?

A. Alison Krauss.

Q. Popular in the 1940s for her novelty numbers, Dorothy Shay was known by what title?

A. The Park Avenue Hillbilly.

Q. What recording artist was born in Pauls Valley, Oklahoma, on November 21, 1933?

A. Jean Shepard.

Q. What occupation did Margo Smith leave to pursue her singing career?

A. Kindergarten teacher.

Q. Jan Howard and Porter Wagoner were both born in what Missouri town?

A. West Plains.

Q. What was Goldie Hill's 1953 Top-5 hit that was a sequel to Ray Price's hit "Don't Let the Stars Get in Your Eyes"?

A. "I Let the Stars Get in My Eyes."

Q. What was the title of Lari White's 1993 debut album?

A. *Lead Me Not.*

Q. In 1970 what single became the first to go number one for Dolly Parton?

A. "Joshua."

Q. For how many weeks did Tammy Wynette's album *Greatest Hits* remain on the charts?

A. Sixty.

Q. Eleanor Johnson is known by what stage name?

A. Cristy Lane.

Q. With more than fifty country singles and about half that many pop hits as of 1996, who is the most successful female pop-country singer to come from Canada?

A. Anne Murray.

Q. Shania Twain wasn't an instant success. In fact, her first album did not sell very well. How high in the charts did her first two singles go?

A. Both "What Made You Say That?" and "Dance with the One That Brought You" peaked at number fifty-five in 1993.

Q. After cowriting "The River" and "She's Every Woman," what native of Los Angeles launched her solo artist career on the Warner Brothers label in 1994?

A. Victoria Shaw.

Q. What female country performer appeared in such movies as *Valley of Blood, Traveling Light*, and *The Country Music Story*?

A. Penny De Haven.

Reba McEntire in the early 1980s signing autographs for fans at a Mercury Records showcase in Dallas, Texas. By January 1983, Reba had her first number-one hit single "Can't Even Get the Blues." Reba set an awards record by being recognized by the CMA as Female Vocalist of the Year for four consecutive years, 1984 through 1987. [PHOTO COURTESY OF SKIP JACKSON]

Q. What is Dolly Parton's middle name?

A. Rebecca.

———◆———

Q. For what two years was Janie Fricke named the CMA Female Vocalist of the Year?

A. 1982 and 1983.

———◆———

Q. In 1981 who was the winner of the first CMA Horizon Award?

A. Terri Gibbs.

———◆———

Q. A 1963 house trailer fire took the life of what country star of the 1940s and 1950s?

A. Texas Ruby.

———◆———

Q. "Teddy Bear Song" and "Kid Stuff" were both Top-5 hits for what performer in 1973?

A. Barbara Fairchild.

Dollywood

Dolly Parton's long-time dream of giving something back to her Smoky Mountain home community was realized when she acquired the Silver Dollar City theme park in Pigeon Forge, Tennessee, just outside of Gatlinburg. She personalized the park with her butterfly logo, the inclusion of some of her family in the music shows, a restaurant called Aunt Granny's (the name her nieces and nephews gave her), a replica of the home where she grew up, and a museum depicting her "rags-to-riches" story. She reopened it as Dollywood in May 1986.

The park's history dates back to 1961. It first opened as Rebel Railroad, a small complex which contained a steam train, a general store, a blacksmith shop, and a saloon. A log flume ride was added in the mid-1960s. In 1970 the park became the property of the Cleveland Browns football team, and was renamed Goldrush Junction. The Browns added a pool, campground, cabins, picnic area, church, barn, wood shop, gristmill, sawmill, outdoor theater, parking lot, and kiddie rides. In 1976 the Herschend family, the owners of Silver Dollar City in Branson, Missouri, bought the park and called it Goldrush. They later changed its name to Silver Dollar City and added more rides and a larger craft area. Dolly has expanded the complex further since 1985, adding shows, rides, restaurants, a bakery, gardens, gift and apparel shops, and special activities for children.

Q. In 1992 what artist served a two-day jail term in Nashville for contempt of court charges arising from a child custody battle?

A. Lynn Anderson.

———◆———

Q. Where in Georgia was Trisha Yearwood born on September 19, 1964?

A. Monticello.

Q. In 1992 what star donated a large grant for liver research to the American Liver Foundation?

A. Naomi Judd.

———◆———

Q. Patty Loveless is distantly related to what veteran country music star?

A. Loretta Lynn.

———◆———

Q. What was Martina McBride's 1992 debut single?

A. "The Time Has Come."

———◆———

Q. What Reba McEntire compact disc was her first album to sell more than two million copies?

A. *For My Broken Heart.*

———◆———

Q. What performer, known as Miss Country Soul, joined *The Grand Ole Opry* on September 16, 1967?

A. Jeannie Seely.

———◆———

Q. Written by Thom Schuyler, the song "Sixteenth Avenue," which has been called the Music Row anthem, was made famous by what singer?

A. Lacy J. Dalton.

———◆———

Q. As a teenager, Patty Loveless first appeared on *The Grand Ole Opry* as a member of whose touring group?

A. The Wilburn Brothers.

Q. Who selected the stage name Tammy for Virginia Wynette Pugh?

A. Billy Sherrill.

◆

Q. What was Mother Maybelle Carter's maiden name?

A. Addington.

◆

Q. With what rock artist and engineer did K. T. Oslin coproduce her 1996 comeback album?

A. Rick Will.

◆

Q. Where did Rosanne Cash record her first album in the summer of 1978?

A. Munich, Germany.

◆

Q. Where was Emmylou Harris born on April 2, 1947?

A. Birmingham, Alabama.

◆

Q. The Capitol label release "Love Was Once around the Dance Floor" made the charts for what artist in 1975?

A. Linda Hargrove.

◆

Q. What is the hometown of Helen Cornelius?

A. Hannibal, Missouri.

◆

Q. Who was the first African American female artist to be a guest on *The Grand Ole Opry*?

A. Linda Martell.

In addition to her vocals, Barbara Mandrell plays bass, banjo, guitar, mandolin, pedal steel, saxophone, and dobro during her stage shows. The multi-talented Texan was born in Houston on Christmas Day 1948. In 1960 Barbara made her first professional appearance by demonstrating pedal steel guitars for Standell Amplifiers at a Chicago music trade show. By age eleven Barbara was a regular on the Los Angeles area Town Hall Party *television show. Barbara has garnered numerous awards from CMA, ACM, NARAS,* Music City News, Radio & Records, Cashbox, *and* Billboard. *"The Battle Hymn of the Republic" is Barbara's favorite song.* [PHOTO COURTESY OF MANDRELL MANAGEMENT]

Q. At what age did Wanda Jackson obtain her own radio show?

A. Thirteen.

———◆———

Q. Patricia Ramey is the maiden name of what performer?

A. Patty Loveless.

———◆———

Q. What disease forced Molly O'Day to retire prematurely in 1952?

A. Tuberculosis.

———◆———

Q. What artist was suspended from *The Grand Ole Opry* in 1973 for criticizing the Metro Nashville Police Department during a live broadcast on WSM?

A. Skeeter Davis.

———◆———

Q. Rosanne Cash's hit single "Tennessee Flat Top Box" was originally released by her father, Johnny Cash, in what year?

A. 1961.

———◆———

Q. What was Helen Cornelius's first single on the RCA label?

A. "We Still Sing Love Songs in Missouri."

———◆———

Q. On June 9, 1984, who became the youngest member of *The Grand Ole Opry*?

A. Lorrie Morgan, then twenty-four.

———◆———

Q. What performer was born Molly Beachwood in Oklahoma City on August 18, 1939?

A. Molly Bee.

Ronna Reeves made her stage debut at age eight by performing in, and winning, the Little Miss Big Springs (Texas) competition. By eleven, Ronna had put together her own band, and at age seventeen she had a stint as the opening act for George Strait. Ronna's The More I Learn *album generated national acclaim with such cuts as "I'll Be Faithful," "Heartbreak Shoes," "Bless Your Cheatin' Heart," and the duet with Sammy Kershaw, "There's Love on the Line."* [BY PERMISSION OF MERCURY/POLYGRAM RECORDS]

Q. What 1985 movie was based on Patsy Cline's career?

A. *Sweet Dreams.*

———◆———

Q. What artist was born Miriam Johnson in Phoenix, Arizona, on May 25, 1947?

A. Jessi Colter.

———◆———

Q. To what rodeo champion was Reba McEntire first married?

A. Charlie Battles.

Illinois native Suzy Bogguss holds a unique degree in metalsmithing. Aces was the title of Suzy's breakthrough album and was followed by her Voices in the Wind project, which she produced with Jimmy Bowen. [BY PERMISSION OF LIBERTY RECORDS]

Q. In the summer of 1987, what K. T. Oslin video went number one on Country Music Television (CMT)?

A. "80's Ladies."

Q. What was the actual name of the 1940s cowgirl yodeling star Rosalie Allen?

A. Julie Marlene Bedra.

Q. With her 1935 release of "I Want to Be a Cowboy's Sweetheart," who became the first female country artist to have a million-selling record?

A. Patsy Montana.

Q. Where was Lynn Anderson born on September 26, 1947?

A. Grand Forks, North Dakota.

Q. Prior to withdrawing her name from competition, Rhonda Vincent was selected as Female Vocalist of the Year in bluegrass music how many times?

A. Five.

Q. Who first gained prominence in Nashville by starring for two years in the lead role of the theatrical presentation of *Always, Patsy Cline*?

A. Mandy Barnett.

Q. How old was Loretta Lynn when she first became a grandmother?

A. Thirty-two.

Q. Who had a big hit single in the mid-1960s with "Queen of the House," a sequel to Roger Miller's "King of the Road"?

A. Jody Miller.

Q. Where was Canadian Anne Murray born on June 20, 1945?

A. Spring Hill, Nova Scotia.

Q. Under what name did Ira Louvin's wife, Florence, perform?

A. Anne Young.

Q. What country artist was born Brenda Mae Tarpley on December 11, 1944, in Atlanta, Georgia?

A. Brenda Lee.

Q. Although the Don Gibson tune "Sweet Dreams" was recorded and charted by several performers, who has been the only artist to take it to number one in the charts?

A. Emmylou Harris.

Q. When were Janie Fricke and Randy Jackson married?

A. September 16, 1982.

Q. In 1977 what single by Crystal Gayle became her first major crossover hit?

A. "Don't It Make My Brown Eyes Blue."

Q. What Big Springs, Texas, native was nominated for the ACM's Top New Female Vocalist in 1991?

A. Ronna Reeves.

Q. What native of Chatham, Ontario, was named by the Canadian Country Music Association as the 1991 Female Vocalist of the Year?

A. Michelle Wright.

Q. Where was Teresa "Terri" Gibbs born?

A. Miami, Florida.

Q. What artist, with such hits as "Someday Soon," "Outbound Plane," and "Somewhere Between," is a native of Aledo, Illinois?

A. Suzy Bogguss.

A prodigy from Illinois, Alison Krauss won the state fiddle championship at age twelve and released her first solo album for Rounder Records before her sixteenth birthday. She's one of a select circle of artists who have won Grammy awards in both the country and bluegrass fields, and she surprised everyone when she took home four CMA awards at the 1995 ceremony. In addition to her fiddle skills, she's a remarkable singer and mandolinist with an unerring eye for adventurous material which she adapts for her ace band Union Station. Her esteem within the industry was underscored by her selection to join The Grand Ole Opry *in 1993, just a month before she turned twenty-two.* [PHOTO PROVIDED BY JOHN LOMAX III]

Q. What was the first solo single of Shelby Lynne, who was voted New Female Vocalist of the Year in 1991 by the ACM?

A. "Under Your Spell Again."

———◆———

Q. In July 1992 what country performer made two appearances on the television soap opera *One Life to Live*?

A. Reba McEntire.

———◆———

Q. Where was Wilma Burgess born on June 11, 1939?

A. Orlando, Florida.

———◆———

Q. What is Texan Billie Jo Spears's actual name?

A. Billie Jean Spears.

Q. Who is Carlene Carter's father?

A. Carl Smith.

———◆———

Q. What breed of dogs does Lacy J. Dalton raise as a hobby?

A. Australian shepherds.

———◆———

Q. Where in Virginia was New Jersey-born Juice (Judy Kay) Newton raised?

A. Virginia Beach.

———◆———

Q. How many number-one and Top-10 hits, respectively, did Donna Fargo enjoy?

A. Six number-one singles and an additional ten Top-10s.

———◆———

Q. What is Holly Dunn's middle name?

A. Suzette.

———◆———

Q. Who had her first chart topper in 1980 with "Who's Cheatin' Who"?

A. Charly McClain.

———◆———

Q. What became Martina McBride's first number-one video on CMT, VH-1, TNN, and CMT Europe?

A. "My Baby Loves Me."

———◆———

Q. Where in Kentucky was Loretta Lynn born on April 14, 1935?

A. Butcher's Hollow.

3

DUOS, TRIOS, AND GROUPS

Q. By what name was Alabama known prior to 1977?

A. Wild Country.

Q. The Ozark Mountain Daredevils evolved from what Springfield, Missouri, band?

A. Cosmic Corncob and His Amazing Mountain Daredevils.

Q. With whom did Moe Bandy team to record the 1979 hit "Just Good Ol' Boys"?

A. Joe Stampley.

Q. Buck Owens formed what band after moving to Bakersfield, California, in 1951?

A. The Schoolhouse Playboys.

Q. Name the three female singers, stars in their own right, who occasionally gather to record as "the Trio."

A. Linda Ronstadt, Emmylou Harris, and Dolly Parton.

Q. What are the first names of the Bellamy Brothers?

A. Howard and David.

———◆———

Q. What harmonica player led the Crook Brothers band on *The Grand Ole Opry* for more than sixty years?

A. Herman Crook.

———◆———

Q. With whom did Willie Nelson record the mid-1980s hit "Seven Spanish Angels"?

A. Ray Charles.

———◆———

Q. What country standard was the first single from the historic collaboration of Tammy Wynette, Dolly Parton, and Loretta Lynn?

A. "Silver Threads and Golden Needles."

———◆———

Q. Garth Brooks was a member of what band in 1979?

A. The Nyle.

———◆———

Q. Who became Highway 101's lead singer in January 1991, following the resignation of Paulette Carlson?

A. Nikki Nelson.

———◆———

Q. What two brothers left the Kentucky HeadHunters in June 1992?

A. Ricky Lee and Doug Phelps, although Doug rejoined in 1996.

Q. Elton Britt and Rosalie Allen had what 1950 duet hit single?

A. "Quicksilver."

———◆———

Q. Who were the regular members of the family trio the Browns?

A. Ella Maxine, Jim Ed, and Bonnie.

———◆———

Q. What West Virginian led the group Barefoot Jerry?

A. Wayne Moss.

———◆———

Q. What leader of the early *Grand Ole Opry* string band the Possum Hunters made his living as a physician?

A. Dr. Humphrey Bate.

———◆———

Q. With what female performer did Carl Belew record the 1971 single "All I Need Is You"?

A. Betty Jean Robinson.

———◆———

Q. How tall are Brooks and Dunn?

A. Brooks: six feet, two inches; Dunn: six feet, four inches.

———◆———

Q. With what Louisiana band did Mary Chapin Carpenter record the Cajun dance tune "Down at the Twist and Shout"?

A. Beausoleil.

———◆———

Q. From what group did Diamond Rio evolve?

A. The Tennessee River Boys.

Q. Most of the original Sawyer Brown band members served as back-up to what singer-songwriter in 1981 and 1982?

A. Don King.

Q. Both Bobby and Sonny, the Osborne Brothers, were born in what Kentucky town?

A. Hyden.

Q. Reba McEntire and Linda Davis had what number-one duet in 1993?

A. "Does He Love You?"

Q. What was the Oak Ridge Boys' first Top-5 hit in the country charts?

A. "Y'all Come Back Saloon."

Q. Asleep at the Wheel performed on the soundtrack of what 1980 film?

A. *Roadie.*

Q. What group derived its name from a name on the side of a panel truck?

A. BlackHawk.

Q. Barefoot Jerry was formed from the remnants of what other group?

A. Area Code 615.

Q. Before the Foggy River Boys' show relocated to Branson, Missouri, where were its headquarters from 1971 to 1974?

A. Kimberling City, Missouri.

———◆———

Q. What trio had the crossover hit "The Three Bells"?

A. The Browns.

———◆———

Q. What artist-owned record label was formed in 1994 by Kieran Kane, Kevin Welch, Tammy Rogers, and Harry Stinson?

A. Dead Reckoning Records.

———◆———

Q. The Bellamy Brothers' 1979 recording of "If I Said You Had a Beautiful Body, Would You Hold It Against Me" received what award from the CMA of Great Britain?

A. Single of the Year.

———◆———

Q. What husband-wife duo of the 1970s had a nationwide hit with their single "Tennessee Birdwalk"?

A. Jack Blanchard and Misty Morgan.

———◆———

Q. What southern California group had a late-1920s hit with the double release of "When the Bloom Is on the Sage" and "Red River Valley"?

A. Beverly Hillbillies.

———◆———

Q. Before becoming known as the Road Dog Band, what was Mark Collie's backing group called?

A. The Collie Dog Band.

Q. Ricky Van Shelton's number-one hit "Rockin' Years" was a 1991 duet with whom?

A. Dolly Parton.

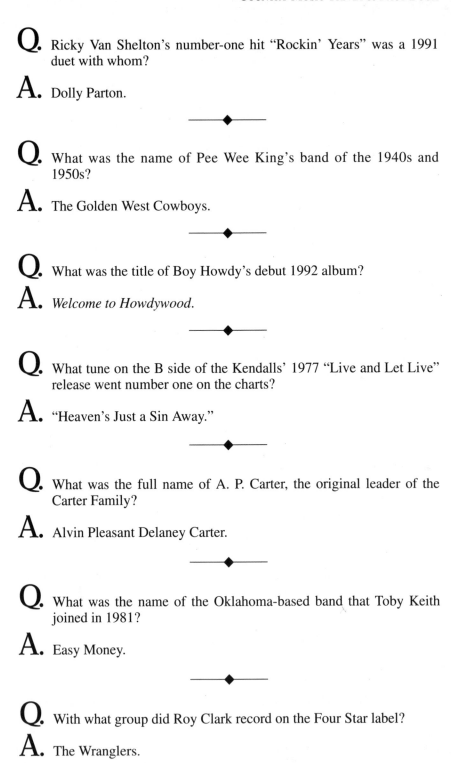

Q. What was the name of Pee Wee King's band of the 1940s and 1950s?

A. The Golden West Cowboys.

Q. What was the title of Boy Howdy's debut 1992 album?

A. *Welcome to Howdywood.*

Q. What tune on the B side of the Kendalls' 1977 "Live and Let Live" release went number one on the charts?

A. "Heaven's Just a Sin Away."

Q. What was the full name of A. P. Carter, the original leader of the Carter Family?

A. Alvin Pleasant Delaney Carter.

Q. What was the name of the Oklahoma-based band that Toby Keith joined in 1981?

A. Easy Money.

Q. With what group did Roy Clark record on the Four Star label?

A. The Wranglers.

George Jones and Tammy Wynette—Mr. and Mrs. Country Music. George and Tammy's tempestuous marriage, which began as a storybook romance in 1968 and ended in a devastating divorce in 1975, was played out in the recording studio as well as in real life. Tammy, born Virginia Wynette Pugh in 1942 in Itawamba County, Mississippi, and raised by her grandparents, grew up working in the cottonfields, dreaming of becoming a singing star. She moved to Nashville in 1966 and was signed that same year by producer Billy Sherrill and Epic Records. Her trademark songs "Stand By Your Man" and "D-I-V-O-R-C-E" were both number-one hits in 1968, the year she married the man already recognized as the greatest living country singer, her idol George Jones. George was born in 1931 in the East Texas town of Saratoga, a densely forested region called the Big Thicket, then moved with his family to Beaumont in 1942. Inspired by Roy Acuff, Bill Monroe, and Hank Williams, Jones's unrestrained and passionate "unearthly voice" remains unparalleled even today. His bouts with the bottle were as famous as his hero Hank Williams's and alcoholism was ultimately responsible for the break-up of his marriage. George and Tammy's recordings, which reflected the evolving stages of their relationship, continued even after they divorced. [PHOTO COURTESY OF ALAN MAYOR]

CMA Vocal Duo of the Year (Introduced in 1970)

1970   Porter Wagoner and Dolly Parton
1971   Porter Wagoner and Dolly Parton
1972   Conway Twitty and Loretta Lynn
1973   Conway Twitty and Loretta Lynn
1974   Conway Twitty and Loretta Lynn
1975   Conway Twitty and Loretta Lynn
1976   Waylon Jennings and Willie Nelson
1977   Jim Ed Brown and Helen Cornelius
1978   Kenny Rogers and Dottie West
1979   Kenny Rogers and Dottie West
1980   Moe Bandy and Joe Stampley
1981   David Frizzell and Shelly West
1982   David Frizzell and Shelly West
1983   Merle Haggard and Willie Nelson
1984   Willie Nelson and Julio Iglesias
1985   Anne Murray and Dave Loggins
1986   Dan Seals and Marie Osmond
1987   Ricky Skaggs and Sharon White
1988   The Judds
1989   The Judds
1990   The Judds
1991   The Judds
1992   Brooks & Dunn
1993   Brooks & Dunn
1994   Brooks & Dunn
1995   Brooks & Dunn

Q. At its peak Bob Wills's Texas Playboys band consisted of how many members?

A. Twenty-one.

———————◆———————

Q. On what program did the Coon Creek Girls appear from 1938 to 1958?

A. *Renfro Valley Barn Dance.*

———————◆———————

Q. "Come Walk with Me," "Big Midnight Special," and "There's a Big Wheel" were all Top-5 hit singles for what husband-wife duo in 1959?

A. Wilma Lee and Stoney Cooper.

Q. What duo had the 1967 hit record "Jackson"?

A. Johnny Cash and June Carter.

———◆———

Q. What were the names of the duo known as the Cochran Brothers from 1954 to 1956?

A. Hank Cochran and Eddie Cochran (no relation to each other).

———◆———

Q. In 1976 what controversial number-one hit by Helen Cornelius and Jim Ed Brown was banned from airplay by some radio stations?

A. "I Don't Want to Have to Marry You."

———◆———

Q. The group Country Gazette evolved from what earlier group?

A. The Flying Burrito Brothers.

———◆———

Q. Name the members of visionary bluegrass group New Grass Revival, as of 1996.

A. Bela Fleck, John Cowan, Pat Flynn, and Sam Bush.

———◆———

Q. In what group did Billy "Crash" Craddock work with his brother Clarence?

A. The Four Rebels.

———◆———

Q. Juice Newton had one duet hit during the 1980s. Name the male singer and the song.

A. Juice and Eddie Rabbitt hit number one in 1986 with "Both to Each Other (Friends and Lovers)."

Q. What was the name of the first group that Dick Curless joined after finishing high school?

A. The Trail Blazers.

Q. Lacy J. Dalton was the lead singer for what psychedelic California rock group?

A. Office.

Q. The Bellamy Brothers' version of what song was a number-one pop hit and a number-twenty-one country hit in 1976?

A. "Let Your Love Flow."

Q. Fiddler supreme Mark O'Connor had two chart singles in 1991 and 1993. Name the vocalists on these records.

A. Steve Wariner, Vince Gill, Ricky Skaggs, Johnny Cash, Marty Stuart, and Travis Tritt for "Restless" and "The Devil Comes Back to Georgia."

Q. With what band did Charlie Daniels most often play from 1958 to 1967?

A. The Jaguars.

Q. How many duet singles by George Jones and Tammy Wynette charted between 1971 and 1980?

A. Thirteen.

Q. Who were the original members of Dave and Sugar?

A. Dave Rowland, Vicki Hackman, and Jackie Frantz.

Q. What was the first release for the Nashville Brass?

A. "I Saw the Light."

Q. BlackHawk leader Henry Paul is an alumnus of what southern rock band?

A. The Outlaws.

Q. The Pirates of the Mississippi had their biggest hit with "Feed Jake." Who was Jake?

A. A dog.

Q. With what band did Jimmy Dean perform in the Washington, D.C., area while he was in the air force?

A. Tennessee Haymakers.

Q. Sam Alldred and DeWayne "Son" Smith are the leaders of what comedy duo?

A. The Geezinslaw Brothers, later changed to the Geezinslaws.

Q. After surviving several years of music industry neglect, Boy Howdy was signed by what label in 1992?

A. Curb Records.

Q. "Mama, She's Lazy" reached number thirty-nine in 1984 for what comedy group?

A. Pinkard and Bowden.

Q. Name the successful vocal collaboration between Lionel Richie and Alabama.

A. "Deep River Woman."

———◆———

Q. What group hit it big in 1996 with "What Do I Know?"

A. Ricochet.

———◆———

Q. What were the actual names of the comic singing duo of Homer and Jethro?

A. Henry D. Haynes and Kenneth C. Burns.

———◆———

Q. What was the name of Doyle Holly's band of the early 1970s?

A. Vanishing Breed.

———◆———

Q. Carl and Pearl Butler appeared in what 1967 movie?

A. *Second Fiddle to a Steel Guitar.*

———◆———

Q. Pedal-steelman Pete Drake formed what band in the early 1950s?

A. Sons of the South.

———◆———

Q. In 1995 what group charted a single for an independent label, was picked up by Curb Records, and went to number ten with "You Have the Right to Remain Silent"?

A. Perfect Stranger.

———◆———

Q. The Jordanaires were formed in 1948 in what Missouri city?

A. Springfield.

Founded as Wildcountry in 1969, Alabama (which they became in 1977) blazed new trails in country music by demonstrating that a self-contained band could be successful. Cousins Randy Owen, Teddy Gentry, and Jeff Cook enlisted drummer Mark Herndon in 1979, then signed with RCA the next year. They hit number one with their first single, "Tennessee River," and have gone gold or platinum with every album they have released. They have won almost every honor in the field, including three CMA nods as Vocal Group of the Year, two victories as Entertainer of the Year, and two Grammys. [DEAN DIXON PHOTO PROVIDED BY RCA RECORDS]

Q. Who sang a duet with Bobby Bare on "No Memories Hangin' 'Round"?

A. Rosanne Cash.

Q. How many of the original members of Little Texas are *not* from the Lone Star State?

A. Two: Brady Seals and Del Gray.

Q. Before its name was changed to Hurricane in 1981, what was the name of Leon Everette's band?

A. Tender Loving Care.

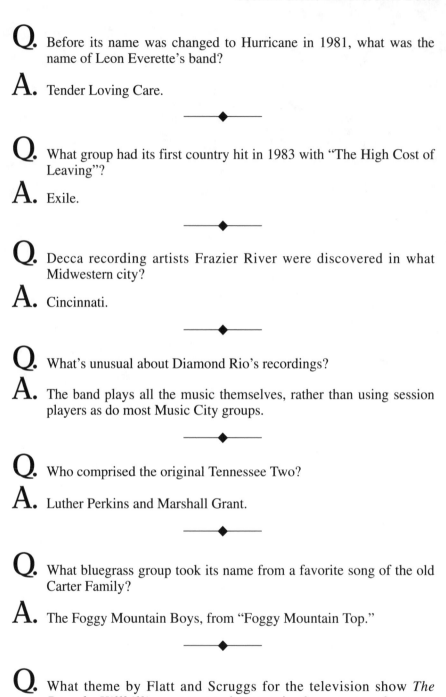

Q. What group had its first country hit in 1983 with "The High Cost of Leaving"?

A. Exile.

Q. Decca recording artists Frazier River were discovered in what Midwestern city?

A. Cincinnati.

Q. What's unusual about Diamond Rio's recordings?

A. The band plays all the music themselves, rather than using session players as do most Music City groups.

Q. Who comprised the original Tennessee Two?

A. Luther Perkins and Marshall Grant.

Q. What bluegrass group took its name from a favorite song of the old Carter Family?

A. The Foggy Mountain Boys, from "Foggy Mountain Top."

Q. What theme by Flatt and Scruggs for the television show *The Beverly Hillbillies* went number one in the country charts on January 19, 1963?

A. "The Ballad of Jed Clampett."

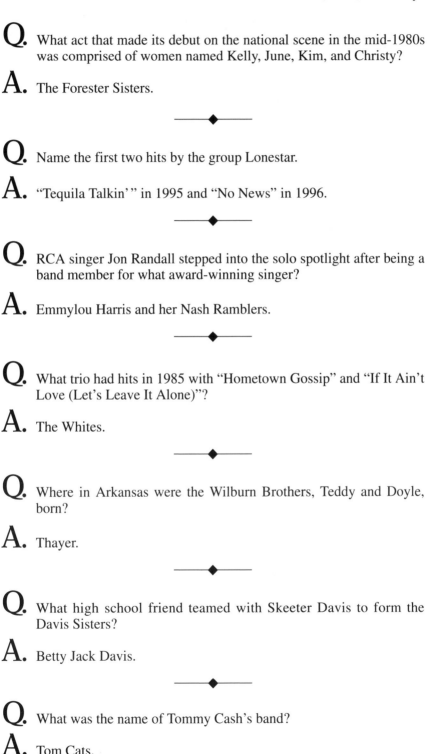

Q. What act that made its debut on the national scene in the mid-1980s was comprised of women named Kelly, June, Kim, and Christy?

A. The Forester Sisters.

Q. Name the first two hits by the group Lonestar.

A. "Tequila Talkin'" in 1995 and "No News" in 1996.

Q. RCA singer Jon Randall stepped into the solo spotlight after being a band member for what award-winning singer?

A. Emmylou Harris and her Nash Ramblers.

Q. What trio had hits in 1985 with "Hometown Gossip" and "If It Ain't Love (Let's Leave It Alone)"?

A. The Whites.

Q. Where in Arkansas were the Wilburn Brothers, Teddy and Doyle, born?

A. Thayer.

Q. What high school friend teamed with Skeeter Davis to form the Davis Sisters?

A. Betty Jack Davis.

Q. What was the name of Tommy Cash's band?

A. Tom Cats.

CMA Vocal Group of the Year

1967	The Stoneman Family	1982	Alabama
1968	Porter Wagoner and	1983	Alabama
	Dolly Parton	1984	The Statler Brothers
1969	Johnny Cash and	1985	The Judds
	June Carter	1986	The Judds
1970	The Glaser Brothers	1987	The Judds
1971	The Osborne Brothers	1988	Highway 101
1972	The Statler Brothers	1989	Highway 101
1973	The Statler Brothers	1990	Kentucky
1974	The Statler Brothers		HeadHunters
1975	The Statler Brothers	1991	Kentucky
1976	The Statler Brothers		HeadHunters
1977	The Statler Brothers	1992	Diamond Rio
1978	The Oak Ridge Boys	1993	Diamond Rio
1979	The Statler Brothers	1994	Diamond Rio
1980	The Statler Brothers	1995	The Mavericks
1981	Alabama		

Q. Janie Fricke joined what Nashville sessions group in the mid-1970s?

A. The Lea Jane Singers.

◆

Q. Who formed the outlandish country rock band the Texas Jewboys?

A. Richard "Kinky" Friedman.

◆

Q. What duet by David Frizzell and Shelly West was a 1981 chart-topper?

A. "You're the Reason God Made Oklahoma."

◆

Q. Larry Gatlin and the Gatlin Brothers band had what number-one hit in 1979?

A. "All the Gold in California."

Q. While they were in high school, Gene, Jerry, and Johnny Gimble, along with James Ivie, formed what group?

A. Rose City Swingsters.

Q. Sisters Dorothy Laverne "Dolly" Good and Mildred Fern "Millie" Good formed what early country duo?

A. Girls of the Golden West.

Q. From 1949 to 1957, what duo had a daily television show in the Chicago area on WNBQ?

A. Lulu Belle and Scotty.

Q. In 1967 who became the front man and emcee for Dottie West's band the Heartaches?

A. Red Lane.

Q. What all-woman band, that included Webb Pierce's daughter, Debbie, tallied seven chart singles in the 1980s?

A. Chantilly.

Q. What popular duo of the 1960s had such hits as "Loving Arms," "Too Late to Try Again," "I'm Hanging Up the Phone," and "Just Thought I'd Let You Know"?

A. Carl and Pearl Butler.

Q. What was the actual last name of the Louvin Brothers?

A. Loudermilk.

Q. With whom did Claude Gray record the duet "Let's Go All the Way" on the Granny White label in 1982?

A. Norma Jean.

Q. Before his successful solo career, Lionel Richie led what hit-making vocal group?

A. The Commodores.

Q. In 1985 Tammy Wynette teamed up with what singer-songwriter to record the Top-10 duet "Sometimes When We Touch"?

A. Mark Gray.

Q. Gail Davies charted a couple of late-1980s records as the leader of what group?

A. Wild Choir.

Q. Name the members of the all-female group Wild Rose, as of 1996.

A. Pamela Gadd, Wanda Vick, Pam Perry, Kathy Mac, and Nancy Given Prout.

Q. What two country superstars teamed up to record the duet album *Pancho & Lefty*?

A. Willie Nelson and Merle Haggard.

Q. How many chart singles did Danny Shirley have before Confederate Railroad hit it big in 1992?

A. Five, the biggest of which was "Love and Let Love," which hit number seventy-two in 1984.

Q. In 1976 what trio had a number-one hit with "The Door Is Always Open"?

A. Dave and Sugar.

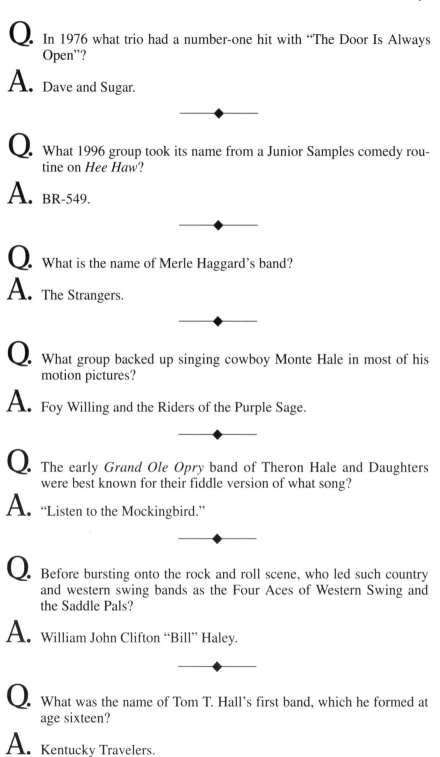

Q. What 1996 group took its name from a Junior Samples comedy routine on *Hee Haw*?

A. BR-549.

Q. What is the name of Merle Haggard's band?

A. The Strangers.

Q. What group backed up singing cowboy Monte Hale in most of his motion pictures?

A. Foy Willing and the Riders of the Purple Sage.

Q. The early *Grand Ole Opry* band of Theron Hale and Daughters were best known for their fiddle version of what song?

A. "Listen to the Mockingbird."

Q. Before bursting onto the rock and roll scene, who led such country and western swing bands as the Four Aces of Western Swing and the Saddle Pals?

A. William John Clifton "Bill" Haley.

Q. What was the name of Tom T. Hall's first band, which he formed at age sixteen?

A. Kentucky Travelers.

Q. Ricky Lee Phelps joined what group upon relocating to Nashville in 1982?

A. Sweetwater.

Q. In 1984 what duo had number-one hits with "Mama, He's Crazy" and "Why Not Me?"

A. The Judds.

Q. What group backed up Red Foley in 1950 on his million-seller version of "Just a Closer Walk with Thee"?

A. The Jordanaires.

Q. In 1976 "Golden Ring" went to the top of the charts for what duo?

A. George Jones and Tammy Wynette.

Q. What bluegrass duo formed and headed the Virginia Boys?

A. Jim and Jesse (McReynolds).

Q. What drummer joined the Tennessee Two in 1960 to create the Tennessee Three?

A. W. S. Holland.

Q. Waylon Jennings formed what band in the early 1960s after relocating to Phoenix, Arizona?

A. The Waylors.

Kentuckians Phil and Don, the Everly Brothers, at home in November 1955. Over the next ten years this young duo saturated the country and pop charts with such megahits as "Bye Bye Love," "Wake Up, Little Susie," "Bird Dog," "All I Have to Do Is Dream," and "Cathy's Clown." [PHOTO COURTESY OF SKIP JACKSON]

Q. What Houston-based jazz combo employed Kenny Rogers in 1959?

A. The Bobby Doyle Trio utilized Rogers as their standup bass player.

◆

Q. When British rocker Elvis Costello made his *Almost Blue* album in Nashville, who were the players who recorded it with him?

A. His own band, the Attractions.

**CMA Instrumental Group of the Year
(Discontinued in 1987)**

1967	The Buckaroos
1968	The Buckaroos
1969	Danny Davis & the Nashville Brass
1970	Danny Davis & the Nashville Brass
1971	Danny Davis & the Nashville Brass
1972	Danny Davis & the Nashville Brass
1973	Danny Davis & the Nashville Brass
1974	Danny Davis & the Nashville Brass
1975	Roy Clark and Buck Trent
1976	Roy Clark and Buck Trent
1977	The Original Texas Playboys
1978	The Oak Ridge Boys Band
1979	The Charlie Daniels Band
1980	The Charlie Daniels Band
1981	Alabama
1982	Alabama
1983	The Ricky Skaggs Band
1984	The Ricky Skaggs Band
1985	The Ricky Skaggs Band
1986	The Oak Ridge Boys Band

Q. During what years was the Harden Trio a member of *The Grand Ole Opry*?

A. 1966 to 1968.

———◆———

Q. What was the name of Ferlin Husky's band?

A. The Hush Puppies.

———◆———

Q. In what year did Flatt and Scruggs separate?

A. 1969.

Q. What was the name of the Nitty Gritty Dirt Band's highly acclaimed 1971 three-record set that included a wide variety of country artists?

A. *Will the Circle Be Unbroken.*

Q. "Why, Baby, Why?" and "Little Rosa" were hit duets in 1955 and 1956, respectively, for what two artists?

A. Webb Pierce and Red Sovine.

Q. In 1972 what duo became the first act to perform at the Rooftop Lounge in Roger Miller's King of the Road motor hotel in Nashville?

A. Jack Greene and Jeannie Seely.

Q. Paul Warmack headed what early *Grand Ole Opry* string band?

A. The Gully Jumpers.

Q. With whom did George Jones record the 1982 duet album *A Taste of Yesterday's Wine*?

A. Merle Haggard.

Q. Name the members of the Texas Tornados, as of 1996.

A. Doug Sahm, Augie Meyers, Flaco Jimenez, and Freddy Fender.

Q. What famed rock band's manager helmed Clint Black's early career, forging his deal with RCA Records?

A. ZZ Top mastermind Bill Ham.

Q. In 1985 what group had a Top-10 hit with their first single "(That's What You Do) When You're in Love"?

A. The Forester Sisters.

Q. How many chart records did Baillie and the Boys craft for RCA from 1987 through 1991?

A. Ten, seven of which made the Top 10.

Q. Singer and picker Jimmy Martin formed what bluegrass group?

A. Sunny Mountain Boys.

Q. Siblings Cal, Don, Fred, Henry, and Rose comprised what act?

A. The Maddox Brothers and Rose.

Q. "After the Fire Is Gone," "Lead Me On," and "Louisiana Woman, Mississippi Man" are among what former duo's number-one hits?

A. Conway Twitty and Loretta Lynn.

Q. Before forming the First Edition and after his time with Bobby Doyle, Kenny Rogers linked up with what other groups?

A. The Kirby Stone Four and the New Christy Minstrels.

Q. What duo recorded the 1983 hit "Paradise Tonight"?

A. Mickey Gilley and Charly McClain.

Q. What group was accused of political incorrectness for their incorporation of the rebel flag in their logo?

A. Confederate Railroad.

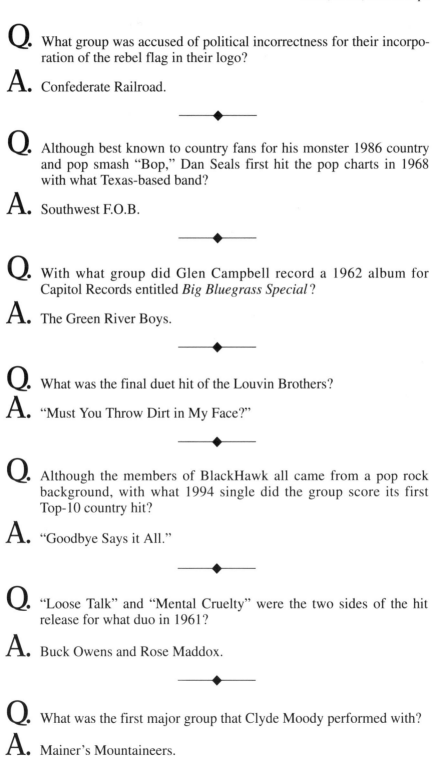

Q. Although best known to country fans for his monster 1986 country and pop smash "Bop," Dan Seals first hit the pop charts in 1968 with what Texas-based band?

A. Southwest F.O.B.

Q. With what group did Glen Campbell record a 1962 album for Capitol Records entitled *Big Bluegrass Special*?

A. The Green River Boys.

Q. What was the final duet hit of the Louvin Brothers?

A. "Must You Throw Dirt in My Face?"

Q. Although the members of BlackHawk all came from a pop rock background, with what 1994 single did the group score its first Top-10 country hit?

A. "Goodbye Says it All."

Q. "Loose Talk" and "Mental Cruelty" were the two sides of the hit release for what duo in 1961?

A. Buck Owens and Rose Maddox.

Q. What was the first major group that Clyde Moody performed with?

A. Mainer's Mountaineers.

Q. In 1991 Estonia became an independent nation. Name the first country act to perform there following Estonia's breakaway from the USSR.

A. The Cactus Brothers.

Q. Betsy Smittle and Ty England came from the band of what country superstar?

A. Garth Brooks's group, Stillwater.

Q. How did the Sweethearts of the Rodeo get their first big break?

A. Sisters Kristine and Janis Oliver won the 1985 Wrangler Country Showdown Talent Contest.

Q. Where did Brooks and Dunn film the video clip for their 1996 smash hit "My Maria"?

A. Outside of Lajitas, Texas, in the area near Big Bend National Park.

Q. With whom did Willie Nelson team in 1984 to record the country and pop hit "To All the Girls I've Loved Before"?

A. Julio Iglesias.

Q. On what label did New Grass Revival record its debut album?

A. Starday.

Q. Jimmy C. Newman formed what band to back him up in the mid-1970s?

A. Cajun Country.

Q. What was the name of Roy Orbison's first band?

A. The Wink Westerners.

Q. The brand name on a box of tissues led to the naming of what group?

A. The Statler Brothers.

Q. Which two members of Hank Williams's Original Drifting Cowboys currently tour with Hank's illegitimate daughter, Jett Williams?

A. Don Helms and Jerry Rivers.

Q. The first chart single for the Mavericks, a Grammy-winning quartet, was their remake of what cherished country classic?

A. "Hey Good Lookin'," a number-one smash for Hank Williams in 1951.

Q. In 1996, a 1960s country rock legend joined a 1970s bluegrass innovator and a 1980s refugee from a country duo to form what band?

A. The Sky Kings: Rusty Young (Poco), John Cowan (Newgrass Revival), and Bill Lloyd (Foster and Lloyd).

Q. For what two years were Dottie West and Kenny Rogers named Best Vocal Duo by the CMA?

A. 1978 and 1979.

A rockin' four-piece combo from Miami, Florida, the Mavericks surprised many industry observers by winning the 1995 CMA Award for Best Vocal Group. Several months later, in early 1996, they took home a Grammy Award in the same category. Led by the soaring tenor of Raul Malo, the band has also developed a solid following in Europe. The group's second and third albums, What a Crying Shame *and* Music for All Occasions, *respectively, hit the Top 10 on the country album charts, with the latter earning platinum certification. Their eclectic, some say "retro," sounds have made them a favorite with rock and country fans alike. From left to right: Robert Reynolds, Paul Deakin, Raul Malo, and Nick Kane.* [PETER NASH PHOTO PROVIDED BY MCA NASHVILLE]

Q. After seven years with MGM, the Osborne Brothers signed with what label in 1963?

A. Decca.

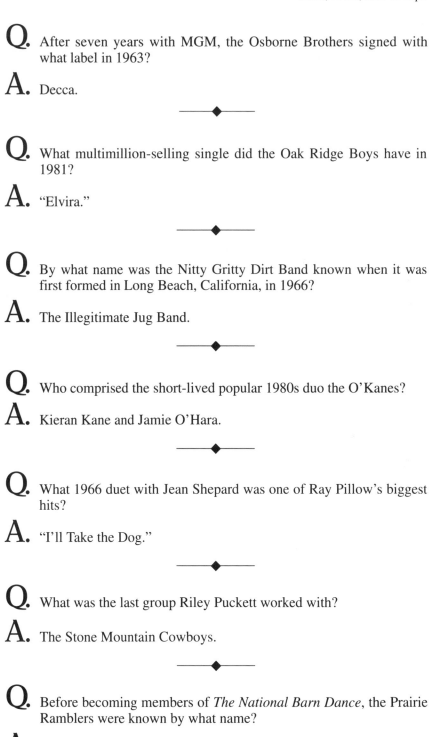

Q. What multimillion-selling single did the Oak Ridge Boys have in 1981?

A. "Elvira."

Q. By what name was the Nitty Gritty Dirt Band known when it was first formed in Long Beach, California, in 1966?

A. The Illegitimate Jug Band.

Q. Who comprised the short-lived popular 1980s duo the O'Kanes?

A. Kieran Kane and Jamie O'Hara.

Q. What 1966 duet with Jean Shepard was one of Ray Pillow's biggest hits?

A. "I'll Take the Dog."

Q. What was the last group Riley Puckett worked with?

A. The Stone Mountain Cowboys.

Q. Before becoming members of *The National Barn Dance*, the Prairie Ramblers were known by what name?

A. The Kentucky Ramblers.

Q. Kenny Price was the lead singer with what group in the mid-1950s on WLW's *Midwestern Hayride* in Cincinnati?

A. The Hometowners.

—◆—

Q. What band did Ray Price get in the 1950s to back him up?

A. The Cherokee Boys.

—◆—

Q. What two chart records did the sometimes raunchy Ethel and the Shameless Hussies have?

A. "One Night Stan" in 1988 and "It's Just the Whiskey Talkin' " in 1989.

—◆—

Q. What was the first single released by Highway 101 after Paulette Carlson rejoined the group in 1995?

A. "Where'd You Get Your Cheatin' From?"

—◆—

Q. Where did the country rock group Pure Prairie League form in 1971?

A. Cincinnati, Ohio.

—◆—

Q. Where was the video filmed for 4 Runner's first release, "Cain's Blood"?

A. Hawaii.

—◆—

Q. What parody of Johnny Horton's "Battle of New Orleans" did Homer and Jethro record in 1959?

A. "The Battle of Camp Kookamonga."

Q. What Grammy-winning western swing band, led by Ray Benson, celebrated its twenty-fifth anniversary in 1996?

A. Asleep at the Wheel.

Q. With what group did Jack Greene first perform on a full-time basis?

A. Cherokee Trio.

Q. Who replaced Lew De Witt following his retirement from the Statler Brothers because of ill health?

A. Jimmy Fortune.

Q. After splitting with his brother Charlie, Bill Monroe formed what group in Little Rock, Arkansas?

A. The Kentuckians.

Q. Following his discharge from the army in 1975, George Strait formed what group?

A. The Ace in the Hole Band.

Q. Before signing with Magnatone Records, Billy Montana was the leader of what band?

A. Billy Montana and the Long Shots.

Q. What southern rock band from South Carolina had country chart records in the 1970s, 1980s, and 1990s?

A. The Marshall Tucker Band.

Q. By what name were the Tenneva Ramblers first known?

A. The Jimmie Rodgers Entertainers.

Q. Hank Thompson formed what band in 1946?

A. The Brazos Valley Boys.

Q. The Glaser Brothers, Tompall, Chuck (Charles), and Jim (James), were all born near what Nebraska town?

A. Spalding.

Q. With whom did Melba Montgomery record the 1963 hit duet "We Must Have Been out of Our Minds"?

A. George Jones.

Q. Members of which two California rock bands came together to form Southern Pacific?

A. John McFee and Keith Knudsen of the Doobie Brothers joined Stu Cook of Creedence Clearwater Revival.

Q. In 1978 Dottie West and Kenny Rogers recorded what number-one hit duet?

A. "Every Time Two Fools Collide."

Q. What group got its name from a street in Nashville?

A. Sawyer Brown.

Q. Under what stage name did the husband and wife team of Scott Wiseman and Myrtle Eleanor Cooper perform?

A. Lulu Belle and Scotty.

Q. What act has won the most Group of the Year honors from the Canadian Country Music Association?

A. The Family Brown (seven times between 1982 and 1989).

Q. With what all-girl western-swing group did Jean Shepard start her career singing and playing bass?

A. Melody Ranch Girls.

Q. They first gained attention as road musicians for David Allan Coe, but these musicians became much wider-known when they formed what group?

A. Confederate Railroad, with Danny Shirley and other Coe alumni.

Q. With whom did T. G. Sheppard record the 1984 duet "Make My Day"?

A. Clint Eastwood.

Q. After working with the Country Gentlemen in Washington, D.C., Ricky Skaggs formed what bluegrass group of his own?

A. Boone Creek.

Q. Arthur "Guitar Boogie" Smith was the leader of what group?

A. The Crackerjacks.

Q. What two performers recorded the duet singles "Cup of Tea" and "While the Feeling's Good"?

A. Margo Smith and Rex Allen Jr.

Q. What group did James Monroe form?

A. The Midnight Ramblers.

———◆———

Q. Following the breakup of his rock group, what artist became known as a Nashville writer who also fronted the zany MCA group Run C&W?

A. Russell Smith, who wrote and recorded "Third Rate Romance" for the Amazing Rhythm Aces.

———◆———

Q. Who portrayed Patsy Cline's drummer in the movie *Sweet Dreams*?

A. Fred Martin, drummer for the Kentucky HeadHunters.

———◆———

Q. Before his breakthrough success with "Love, Me" in 1992, Collin Raye charted several records as a part of what group?

A. The Wray Brothers Band—later, the Wrays.

———◆———

Q. Prior to joining *The Johnny Cash Show* in the early 1960s, the Statler Brothers performed under what name?

A. The Kingsmen.

———◆———

Q. Prior to 1982 the Whites performed under what name?

A. Buck White and the Down Home Folks.

———◆———

Q. Who led the popular *Grand Ole Opry* band of the 1940s called the Georgia Peach Pickers?

A. Curly Williams.

Hee-Haw

Inspired by the comedy and music of the TV show *Rowan and Martin's Laugh-In, Hee Haw* was first planned by CBS-TV as a summer replacement series. However, when the network decided to drop the Smothers Brothers, *Hee Haw* was recast as a prime-time weekly show, premiering on June 15, 1969, with Buck Owens, Roy Clark, Grandpa Jones, Archie Campbell, Junior Samples, the Hager Twins, Minnie Pearl, and guest stars Charley Pride and Loretta Lynn. The show was dropped by CBS in 1971, but was syndicated that same year.

The *Hee Haw* comedy skits, placed in rural settings such as cornfields, barnyards, around a pot-bellied stove in a general store, or in front of a rickety cabin, drew their humor from modern gagwriters as well as vaudeville, burlesque, minstrel sources, and early hillbilly comic tradition. Although many complained that *Hee Haw* presented a hayseed-buffoon image of country music and rural life that the performers had been resisting for years, the longevity of the show has confounded all the critics.

One of the series' most popular acts, the Hee Haw Gospel Quartet, featured Grandpa Jones, Roy Clark, Buck Owens, and Kenny Price in virtuoso vocal and instrumental harmonic performances of traditional gospel favorites.

Other cast members have included Stringbean, Sheb Wooley, Jerry Clower, Gordie Tapp, Marianne Gordon Rogers, Roni Stoneman, Misty Rowe, and Irlene Mandrell.

Q. Don Williams was a member of what pop-folk group during the 1960s?

A. The Pozo Seco Singers.

———◆———

Q. What was the name of Hank Williams's band?

A. The Drifting Cowboys.

Q. At what Murfreesboro, Tennessee, facility did the Judds perform their farewell concert in December 1991?

A. Murphy Center at Middle Tennessee State University.

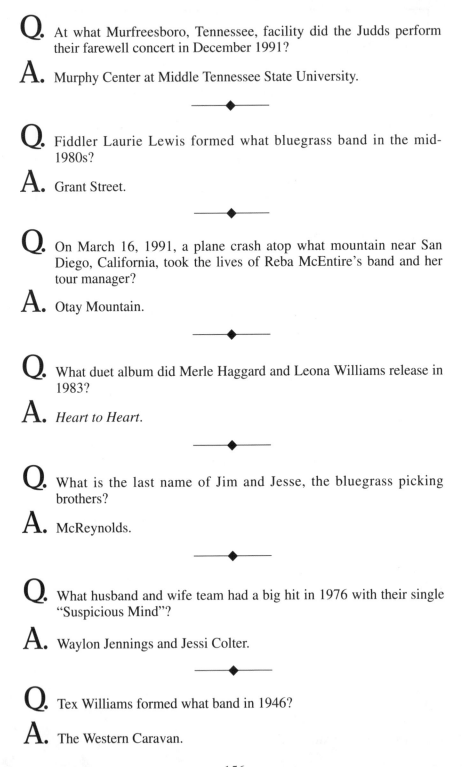

Q. Fiddler Laurie Lewis formed what bluegrass band in the mid-1980s?

A. Grant Street.

Q. On March 16, 1991, a plane crash atop what mountain near San Diego, California, took the lives of Reba McEntire's band and her tour manager?

A. Otay Mountain.

Q. What duet album did Merle Haggard and Leona Williams release in 1983?

A. *Heart to Heart.*

Q. What is the last name of Jim and Jesse, the bluegrass picking brothers?

A. McReynolds.

Q. What husband and wife team had a big hit in 1976 with their single "Suspicious Mind"?

A. Waylon Jennings and Jessi Colter.

Q. Tex Williams formed what band in 1946?

A. The Western Caravan.

The Oaks trace their beginnings to the gospel group Oak Ridge Quartet, founded in 1945. Over the years the group persevered, enduring numerous personnel changes before becoming the Oak Ridge Boys in 1961. They had their first big secular hit in 1977 with "Y'all Come Back Saloon," kicking off a consistent twelve-year run of hits led by "Elvira," the CMA Single of the Year in 1981 and a pop Top 5. Composed of Joe Bonsall, Duane Allen, Richard Sterban, and William Lee Golden for most of the Oaks' hit-making years, Steve Sanders replaced Golden in 1986, but Golden returned ten years later, taking his old spot with Sanders moving on. The Oaks won numerous CMA and ACM awards in addition to five Grammys, four for their gospel work and one for "Elvira." Photo taken before Golden returned to the group in 1996 shows, left to right: Joe Bonsall, Duane Allen, Steve Sanders, and Richard Sterban. [PHOTO PROVIDED BY JOHN LOMAX III]

Q. Who founded the Riders of the Purple Sage in 1940?

A. Foy Willing (Willingham).

———◆———

Q. How much money did Sawyer Brown win on their 1984 appearances on the television talent show *Star Search*?

A. One hundred thousand dollars.

Q. With whom did fourteen-year-old Hank Williams form the duo of the Drifting Cowboys?

A. Smith "Hezzy" Adair.

———◆———

Q. What group's debut, self-named CD on the Arista label went platinum in 1994?

A. The Tractors.

———◆———

Q. In 1956 what release on the Decca label became the Wilburn Brothers' first Top-10 single?

A. "I'm So in Love with You."

———◆———

Q. In the 1970s Vince Gill played with what West Coast bluegrass group headed by Byron Berline?

A. Sundance.

———◆———

Q. What was the title of Brooks and Dunn's debut album (also a single title)?

A. *Brand New Man.*

———◆———

Q. At what Nashville cafe was the cover picture of Sawyer Brown's tenth album *Cafe on the Corner* shot?

A. Mack's Cafe.

———◆———

Q. What band backed Lyle Lovett on his first recording session at an Arizona studio in the mid-1980s?

A. J. David Sloan Band.

Q. What was the name of Carl and Pearl Butler's Franklin, Tennessee, ranch?

A. Cross Over Acres.

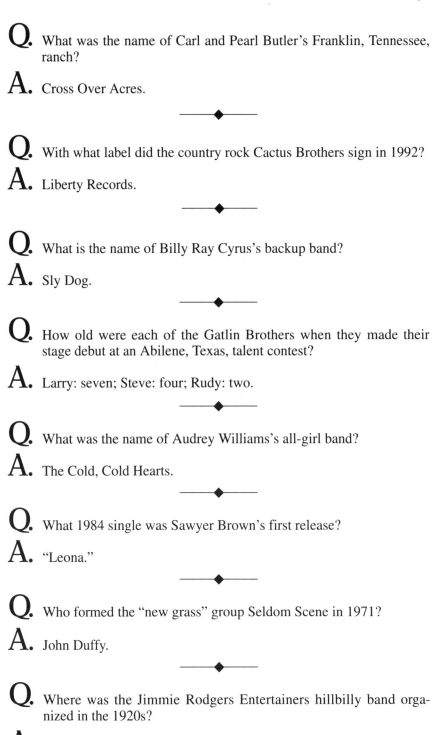

Q. With what label did the country rock Cactus Brothers sign in 1992?

A. Liberty Records.

Q. What is the name of Billy Ray Cyrus's backup band?

A. Sly Dog.

Q. How old were each of the Gatlin Brothers when they made their stage debut at an Abilene, Texas, talent contest?

A. Larry: seven; Steve: four; Rudy: two.

Q. What was the name of Audrey Williams's all-girl band?

A. The Cold, Cold Hearts.

Q. What 1984 single was Sawyer Brown's first release?

A. "Leona."

Q. Who formed the "new grass" group Seldom Scene in 1971?

A. John Duffy.

Q. Where was the Jimmie Rodgers Entertainers hillbilly band organized in the 1920s?

A. Asheville, North Carolina.

Q. What Chicano guitar picker became a member of Tom T. Hall's Storytellers in 1971?

A. Johnny Rodriguez.

Q. Who recorded the number-one country and pop duet "Islands in the Stream" with Kenny Rogers?

A. Dolly Parton.

Q. What legendary gospel quartet sang the closing song at Hank Williams's funeral?

A. The Statesmen.

Q. With what record label did Johnnie Lee Wills and His Boys sign in 1940?

A. Bullet Records.

Q. What was the name of Johnny and Jack's band?

A. Tennessee Mountain Boys.

Q. Who formed the Cumberland Ridge Runners of *National Barn Dance* fame?

A. John Lair.

Q. The bluegrass duo of Mitchell and Everett, the Lilly Brothers, was first known by what name?

A. The Lonesome Holler Boys.

*The Judds (l to r) TV and film actress Ashley, mother Naomi, Wynonna. Both Naomi (Diana Ellen Judd) and Wynonna (Christina Claire Ciminella), mother and daughter, were born in rural Ashland, Kentucky, in 1946 and 1964, respectively. While Naomi was raised listening to traditional country music, Wynonna (who grew up in Los Angeles) had her tastes tempered by California's pop-rock contemporary performers. The Judds began singing at home together, mimicking every country duet they could find, until one of their demo tapes found its way to RCA Records in Nashville in 1983. An audition was scheduled, and the Judds were signed to the label on the spot. Their first number-one record was "Mama, He's Crazy" in 1984. In the fall of 1990, Naomi announced that due to health reasons, she would be retiring from performing, and their final concert, a pay-per-view cable television special, took place on December 4, 1991, on the Middle Tennessee State University campus in Murfreesboro. [*PHOTO COURTESY OF ALAN MAYOR*]*

Q. Dave Rowland, of Dave and Sugar fame, and Richard Sterban, of the Oak Ridge Boys, are both former members of what famous gospel group?

A. J. D. Sumner and the Stamps Quartet.

Q. How many consecutive CMA awards for (Vocal Group) Duo of the Year did the Judds receive?

A. Seven.

Q. What group had such hits as "You Can't Have Your Kate and Edith, Too," "Bed of Roses," and "Class of '57"?

A. The Statler Brothers.

Q. In the mid-1960s what band did Wynn Stewart organize?

A. The Tourists.

Q. Who was the leader of the Blue Ridge Corn Shuckers?

A. Ernest V. "Pop" Stoneman.

Q. What western-oriented trio joined *The Grand Ole Opry* in 1982?

A. Riders in the Sky.

Q. Before relocating to Nashville, Martina McBride belonged to what country act?

A. The Fowler Brothers.

Q. What is the name of Alan Jackson's backup band?

A. The Strayhorns.

Q. The Judds' album *Love Can Build a Bridge* sold how many copies?

A. The album was certified platinum for sales of more than one million copies.

———◆———

Q. What group had the video and single "A Street Man Named Desire"?

A. Pirates of the Mississippi.

———◆———

Q. What longtime Branson, Missouri, group received its original name from the nickname of the Cumberland River?

A. The Foggy River Boys.

———◆———

Q. What vocal backup group is credited with inventing the Nashville number system widely used in recording sessions?

A. The Jordanaires.

———◆———

Q. Jack Anglin of Johnny and Jack fame was killed in a car wreck on his way to the memorial service of what country star?

A. Patsy Cline.

———◆———

Q. Where were the identical twins Jim and John, the Hagers of *Hee Haw* fame, born?

A. Chicago, Illinois.

———◆———

Q. What artists teamed to record the 1984 Top-10 duet single "All Tangled Up in Love"?

A. Earl Thomas Conley and Gus Hardin.

Q. Dennis Robbins sang lead and played slide guitar with what short-lived Warner Brothers recording group?

A. Billy Hill.

———◆———

Q. B. B. Watson was the lead singer with what Texas-Louisiana honky-tonk band?

A. The Gulf Coast Boys.

———◆———

Q. Country recording artist Rich Grissom dropped out of high school to play with what rock band?

A. Champs.

———◆———

Q. Other than country music, what music genres has Marty Stuart worked in?

A. Gospel, folk, and bluegrass.

———◆———

Q. How much time went by between the Geezinslaw Brothers' chart hits "Chubby (Please Take Your Love to Town)" and "Help, I'm White and I Can't Get Down"?

A. Twenty-four years, eight months.

———◆———

Q. Claude Gray organized what band in the mid-1960s?

A. The Graymen.

———◆———

Q. In what year did the three Glaser Brothers split for the first time?

A. 1973.

Throwbacks to the era of the untamed West, Waylon Jennings and Willie Nelson are considered country music's modern-day cowboys. Willie Hugh Nelson, born on April 30, 1933, in Abbott, Texas, and raised by his grandparents in the tiny town of Abbott, was playing guitar in a polka band together with his sister, Bobbie, by the age of ten. Waylon Jennings, born across the state in Littlefield, near the Texas panhandle, on June 15, 1937, had his own radio show at age twelve and was a disk jockey in Lubbock by the time he was fourteen. When Willie and Waylon met in Phoenix in 1965, they both were newly signed to the RCA label. In 1976, together with Waylon's wife, Jessi Colter, and Tompall Glaser, they released an album titled Wanted: The Outlaws, *which became the first country LP in history to sell one million copies. That same year they dominated the CMA awards, awakening the traditional Nashville establishment to the broad appeal of their progressive, no-frills style of country music.* [PHOTO COURTESY OF ALAN MAYOR]

Q. In 1954 what two duet singles were hits for Goldie Hill and Justin Tubb?

A. "Looking Back to See" and "Sure Fire Kisses."

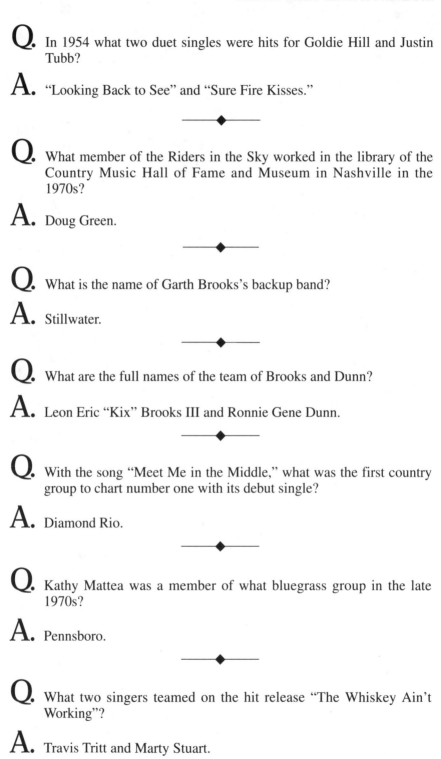

Q. What member of the Riders in the Sky worked in the library of the Country Music Hall of Fame and Museum in Nashville in the 1970s?

A. Doug Green.

Q. What is the name of Garth Brooks's backup band?

A. Stillwater.

Q. What are the full names of the team of Brooks and Dunn?

A. Leon Eric "Kix" Brooks III and Ronnie Gene Dunn.

Q. With the song "Meet Me in the Middle," what was the first country group to chart number one with its debut single?

A. Diamond Rio.

Q. Kathy Mattea was a member of what bluegrass group in the late 1970s?

A. Pennsboro.

Q. What two singers teamed on the hit release "The Whiskey Ain't Working"?

A. Travis Tritt and Marty Stuart.

Q. Pam Tillis formed what jazz-rock combo during her sojourn in San Francisco in the 1970s?

A. Freeflight.

Q. In 1989 what high-tech hit single and hit video featured Hank Williams Jr. singing with his deceased father, Hank Williams Sr.?

A. "There's a Tear in My Beer."

Q. What was the title of Alabama's first album with RCA Records?

A. *My Home's in Alabama.*

Q. What name did Bill Anderson give to his band?

A. Po' Boys.

Q. Made up of Nashville and Muscle Shoals session musicians, the group Area Code 615 recorded two albums on what label?

A. Polydor.

Q. What Ricky Van Shelton and Dolly Parton duet was the top video on CMT for 1991?

A. "Rockin' Years."

Q. Facing trademark litigation from three other groups with the same name, what group filed Chapter 11 bankruptcy in 1991?

A. Shenandoah.

Country Music Television

Another subsidiary of the Gaylord Entertainment Company's Opryland complex, Country Music Television (CMT) went on the air on March 6, 1983, twenty-four hours before The Nashville Network was launched. It premiered July 1984 in Canada and November 1992 in Europe. The brainchild of Glenn Dean "Big Daddy" Daniels, CMT was originally owned by the Telstar Corporation of Beverly Hills. The operation began with five thousand clips, 70 percent of which were shot by the producers, with the record companies furnishing the rest. CMT is on the air twenty-four hours a day, presenting straight video clips with no presiding video jockeys. In February 1993, subscriber count totaled twenty million households in the U.S., Canada, and Europe.

Q. What group has had such hits as "She Took It like a Man," "Jesus and Mama," and "Queen of Memphis"?

A. Confederate Railroad.

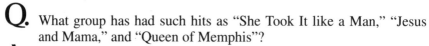

Q. Who sang with Dwight Yoakam on the number-one duet "The Streets of Bakersfield"?

A. Buck Owens.

Q. What country duo rode a float in the 1973 Macy's Thanksgiving Day parade?

A. George Jones and Tammy Wynette.

Q. What was the title of Exile's second Epic album, released in 1984?

A. *Kentucky Hearts.*

Q. What was the CMA's Group of the Year in 1988 and 1989?

A. Highway 101.

———◆———

Q. Who replaced the Phelps brothers in the Kentucky HeadHunters?

A. Mark Orr and Anthony Kenney.

———◆———

Q. What group derived its name from a community in Williamson County, Tennessee?

A. Little Texas.

———◆———

Q. What Australian country duo had a number-one album in Canada entitled *Twincerely Yours*?

A. The Legarde Twins.

———◆———

Q. Howard of the Bellamy Brothers was a member of what law enforcement agency for one day?

A. The FBI.

———◆———

Q. When recording gospel music, Uncle Dave Macon used what name for his group, the Fruit Jar Drinkers?

A. Dixie Sacred Singers.

———◆———

Q. The 1991 Grammy for Best Mexican American Performance went to what group in 1992?

A. The Texas Tornados.

Three-time Grammy winners, Virginia's Statler Brothers are the most-honored vocal group in country music history, taking home top CMA honors ten times, including nine years in a row (1972 through 1980). Brothers Harold and Don Reid joined Phil Balsley and Lew DeWitt to form the group in 1960, becoming the Statler Brothers in 1963. Their first big hit "Flowers on the Wall," written by DeWitt, became a pop and country smash. They followed up with hit singles steadily through the 1980s. Jimmy Fortune joined the band in 1982 when DeWitt's health deteriorated. By the time the 1990s rolled around, the group had lost their radio appeal, but they maintained their popularity through their very popular variety series on TNN. Left to right: Jimmy Fortune, Harold Reid, Don Reid, and Phil Balsley. [JIM HAGANS PHOTO PROVIDED BY MERCURY/POLYGRAM]

Q. Who recorded "It Wasn't You, It Wasn't Me," with Daniele Alexander?

A. Butch Baker.

◆

Q. Who shared with Marie Osmond the CMA's 1986 Duet of the Year award for "Meet Me in Montana?"

A. Dan Seals.

Q. *Bigger Than the Both of Us* is the title of what duo's debut album with Epic Records?

A. Darryl and Don Ellis.

———◆———

Q. What was Great Plains's first single?

A. "A Picture of You."

———◆———

Q. What trio's debut album with Columbia Records was entitled *The Power of Love*?

A. Matthews, Wright, and King.

———◆———

Q. What duo is comprised of Kristine Arnold (Kristine Oliver) and Janis Gill (Janis Oliver)?

A. Sweethearts of the Rodeo.

———◆———

Q. In what year did the Riders in the Sky first perform?

A. 1977.

———◆———

Q. Although they recorded under the name of Shenandoah from their inception, the group was originally incorporated under what name?

A. Diamond Rio.

———◆———

Q. What group performed a series of commercials for Bryan Meats?

A. Alabama.

While much has been said about their look-alike facial features, it was more a case of hero worship that lent the dynamism to the Roy Rogers-Clint Black duet and video "Hold On Partner" in 1991. Clint Patrick Black was born in 1962, five years after Rogers's TV western series went off the air. Black, the youngest of four brothers, was born in Long Branch, New Jersey, and was raised in Texas. He spent most of the 1980s living a hand-to-mouth existence on the rowdy Houston club circuit before being signed to the RCA label in 1988. Roy Rogers, born Leonard Slye on November 5, 1911, in Cincinnati, Ohio, grew up on a small farm in southern Ohio. The crash of 1929 sent Len and his father to California to work as migratory fruit pickers, and it was there that Len Slye turned to a career in music. He formed the Sons of the Pioneers (originally the Pioneer Trio) in 1933 with Bob Nolan and Tim Spencer, and later the brothers Hugh and Karl Farr joined the group. In 1937 Len left the Pioneers to pursue a career as a cowboy actor with Republic Pictures and changed his name first to Dick Weston, then to Roy Rogers. His more than eighty westerns through the 1940s and early 1950s, in addition to his highly popular TV western series from 1951 to 1957 with his wife, Dale Evans, earned him the title King of the Cowboys. He is the only twice-elected member of the Country Music Hall of Fame—once for the Sons of the Pioneers and again as an individual. [PHOTO COURTESY OF ALAN MAYOR]

Q. Where do the Statler Brothers host an annual Fourth of July celebration?

A. Staunton, Virginia.

Q. What reptilian-named Texas band records for Flying Fish Records?

A. The Austin Lounge Lizards.

Q. In 1986 who became the first performers based in Branson, Missouri, to appear on *The Grand Ole Opry*?

A. The Lowe Sisters.

Q. What group, formed in 1984, was named 1989 Top Vocal Group in 1990 by the ACM?

A. Restless Heart.

Q. What EMI recording group from eastern Canada has performed before England's Queen Elizabeth II?

A. The Rankin Family.

Q. What was the name of the Kentucky HeadHunter's longtime mascot at their practice house?

A. Honey, a dog.

Q. On what label did Palomino Road release their self-titled debut album?

A. Liberty Records.

Q. What video by the Pirates of the Mississippi was recognized by *Music Row* magazine as Best Video by a Group in 1991?

A. "Feed Jake."

Q. Jason Ringenberg formed what country rock-cowpunk band?

A. Jason and the Scorchers.

Q. In 1979 what original member of the Sons of the Pioneers recorded the acclaimed solo album *Sound of a Pioneer*?

A. Bob Nolan.

Q. What group was formed at the farm of Ray Benson near Paw Paw, West Virginia?

A. Asleep at the Wheel.

Q. Released in 1979, *Saddle Tramp* was what group's first album on the Epic label?

A. The Charlie Daniels Band.

4

PICKERS, COMICS, WRITERS, AND SONGS

Q. What country humorist and *Grand Ole Opry* star was honored in 1992 by the Mississippi state legislature's renaming of a portion of Mississippi Highway 24 for him?

A. Jerry Clower.

◆

Q. Dolly Parton was inspired by a name on a photo from a young fan to write what song?

A. "Jolene."

◆

Q. What was the title of Chet Atkins's first solo album, released in 1953?

A. *Chet Atkins' Gallopin' Guitar.*

◆

Q. "Make the World Go Away," a big hit for both Eddy Arnold and Ray Price, was written by what songwriter?

A. Hank Cochran.

Q. What unique musical instrument does Curb recording artist Junior Brown play?

A. A "guit-steel," a combination electric and steel guitar.

Q. Bobby Bare's recording of his composition "All-American Boy" was marketed under what name by Fraternity Records in 1958?

A. Bill Parsons.

Q. Name the title and writers of George Strait's first hit in 1981.

A. "Unwound," written by Dean Dillon and Frank Dycus.

Q. What Dallas Frazier tune, inspired by a street name in the Nashville suburb of Inglewood, Tennessee, was a hit for the Oak Ridge Boys in the mid-1960s?

A. "Elvira."

Q. Alex Harvey's "Delta Dawn" was a 1972 Top-10 hit for what recording artist?

A. Tanya Tucker.

Q. Chip Taylor had five charted country singles in the late 1970s, but he's better known for writing what rock anthem?

A. "Wild Thing," a number-one hit for the Troggs in 1966.

Q. What country comedian came to national attention with his mid-1960s recording "Chit Atkins, Make Me a Star"?

A. Don Bowman.

Chester Burton Atkins was born June 20, 1924, in Luttrell, Tennessee, in the Clinch Mountains. The son of a pianist and voice teacher and descendant of a family of old-time fiddlers, Chet began his career playing guitar and fiddle with Archie Campbell and Bill Carlisle over WNOX radio in Knoxville. In the late 1940s, he began touring with the Carter Family, moved with them to Nashville, and soon signed a record contract with RCA. By the early 1950s, he was RCA executive Steve Sholes's assistant, and in 1957 was named A&R for RCA's country division in Nashville. A driving force in the development of the Nashville Sound, for which he credits the versatility of the laid-back southern musicians, it was not until the early 1980s that Chet was able to leave session direction and resume his own career as a performing artist. [PHOTO COURTESY OF ALAN MAYOR]

CMA Song of the Year

1967 "There Goes My Everything"/Dallas Frazier
1968 "Honey"/Bobby Russell
1969 "Carroll County Accident"/Bob Ferguson
1970 "Sunday Morning Coming Down"/Kris Kristofferson
1971 "Easy Loving"/Freddie Hart
1972 "Easy Loving"/Freddie Hart
1973 "Behind Closed Doors"/Kenny O'Dell
1974 "Country Bumpkin"/Don Wayne
1975 "Back Home Again"/John Denver
1976 "Rhinestone Cowboy"/Larry Weiss
1977 "Lucille"/Roger Bowling and Hal Bynum
1978 "Don't It Make My Brown Eyes Blue"/Richard Leigh
1979 "The Gambler"/Don Schlitz/Writers Night Music
1980 "He Stopped Loving Her Today"/Bobby Braddock and Curly Putman/Tree Publishing
1981 "He Stopped Loving Her Today"/Bobby Braddock and Curly Putman/Tree Publishing
1982 "Always on My Mind"/Johnny Christopher, Wayne Carson, Mark James/Screen Gems, EMI Music, Rose Bridge Music
1983 "Always on My Mind"/Johnny Christopher, Wayne Carson, Mark James/Screen Gems, EMI Music, Rose Bridge Music
1984 "Wind beneath My Wings"/Larry Henley, Jeff Silbar/Warner House of Music
1985 "God Bless the U.S.A."/Lee Greenwood/Music Corp. of America, Sycamore Valley Music
1986 "On the Other Hand"/Paul Overstreet, Don Schlitz/Writers Group Music, Scarlet Moon Music, MCA Music and Don Schlitz Music
1987 "Forever and Ever, Amen"/Paul Overstreet, Don Schlitz/Writers Group Music, Scarlet Moon Music, MCA Music and Don Schlitz Music
1988 "80's Ladies"/K.T. Oslin/Wooden Wonder Music
1989 "Chiseled in Stone"/Max D. Barnes, Vern Gosdin/ Hidden Lake Music, Hookem Music
1990 "Where've You Been"/Jon Vezner, Don Henry
1991 "When I Call Your Name"/Vince Gill, Tim DuBois
1992 "Look at Us"/Vince Gill, Max D. Barnes
1993 "I Still Believe in You"/Vince Gill, John Barlow Jarvis
1994 "Chattahoochee"/Alan Jackson, Jim McBride
1995 "Independence Day"/Gretchen Peters

Q. Singer-songwriter Ed Bruce played what character in the 1981–82 television show *Bret Maverick*?

A. Tom Guthrie.

Q. Lloyd Green's first Nashville recording session was for what George Jones single?

A. "Too Much Water."

Q. Who was Faron Young's steelman from 1969 to 1975?

A. Lloyd "Skip" Jackson.

Q. What 1975 Ronnie Milsap release was written by John Schweers?

A. "Daydreams about Night Things."

Q. Roy Acuff's Columbia recording of what song was a million seller in 1942?

A. "Wabash Cannonball."

Q. This writer-artist wrote "Pancho and Lefty" and "If I Needed You" and consistently tours Europe. Name him.

A. Townes Van Zandt.

Q. With whom did Merle Haggard cowrite "Today I Started Loving You Again"?

A. Bonnie Owens.

Q. Who wrote Carl Smith's 1953 chart-buster "Hey Joe"?

A. Boudleaux and Felice Bryant.

Q. What plaid-clad comic was a longtime member of Porter Wagoner's show?

A. Speck Rhodes.

Q. What John Hartford composition became a 1968 gold single for Glen Campbell?

A. "Gentle on My Mind."

Q. What Bobby Helms hit stayed on the charts longer than any country single in history?

A. "Fraulein."

Q. Who wrote and recorded the number-one hit "Seven Year Ache" in the early 1980s?

A. Rosanne Cash.

Q. Dickey Lee has had dozens of hits both as an artist and as a writer. Name the most successful song he has written.

A. "She Thinks I Still Care" hit number one in 1962 for George Jones and number one again in 1974 for Anne Murray as "He Thinks I Still Care."

Q. Which famed songwriter's wife wrote "I'll Be Your San Antone Rose," "Hard Dog to Keep Under the Porch," and "Quarter Moon in a Ten Cent Town"?

A. Susanna Clark, wife of writer-artist Guy Clark.

Q. Tanya Tucker's hit single "Would You Lay with Me in a Field of Stone," and Johnny Paycheck's "Take This Job and Shove It" were both written by what Akron, Ohio, native?

A. David Allan Coe.

Q. By what pet name does comedian and banjo picker Mike Snider refer to his wife?

A. Sweetie.

Q. The 1981 single "Leonard," written and recorded by Merle Haggard, was about what country music personality?

A. Leonard Raymond Sipes (Tommy Collins).

Q. Who composed such hits as Neal McCoy's "Wink," Kathy Mattea's "Walking Away a Winner," Faith Hill's "Take Me as I Am," and Pam Tillis's "Cleopatra Queen of Denial"?

A. Bob DiPiero.

Q. Ace country session players Richard Bennett (guitarist), Glen Worf (bass player), and Paul Franklin (pedal steel player) have toured with what British guitar legend?

A. Mark Knopfler.

Q. Where was piano great Floyd Cramer born on October 27, 1933?

A. Shreveport, Louisiana.

Q. What song recorded by Vernon Dalhart in 1924 sold more than six million discs for Victor Records?

A. "The Wreck of the Old '97."

Q. What steel guitar man majored in psychology for two years at the University of Southern Mississippi?

A. Lloyd Green.

Q. What singer-songwriter composed such songs as "You Are My Sunshine," "Sweethearts or Strangers," and "Nobody's Darlin' but Mine"?

A. Jimmie Davis.

Q. Mac Davis wrote what major Elvis Presley hit?

A. "In the Ghetto."

Q. Whom did singer-songwriter Chuck Cannon wed in April 1994?

A. Lari White.

Q. "One Has My Name, the Other Has My Heart" and "I Dreamed of a Hillbilly Heaven" were cowritten by what Posey, Texas, native?

A. Eddie Dean (Edgar Dean Glossup).

Q. What song written and recorded by Jimmy Dean became certified gold on December 14, 1961?

A. "Big Bad John."

DeFord Bailey, the Harmonica Wizard and one of The Grand Ole Opry's *earliest stars, was born in 1900 in rural Smith County, Tennessee, the son of a freed slave who had fought for the Union army during the Civil War. He learned "black hillbilly music" from a number of his family members and began playing the harmonica when he was just a few years old. In 1925, while working for radio station WDAD in Nashville, George D. Hay, the Solemn Ole Judge, heard him and invited him to join the cast of WSM's new barn dance show. It was DeFord's harmonica performance of "The Pan American Blues," following the classical* Musical Appreciation Hour, *that inspired Hay to announce, on December 10, 1927, "For the past hour we have been listening to music taken largely from grand opera, but from now on we will present* The Grand Ole Opry." [PHOTO COURTESY OF LES LEVERETT]

Grammy Awards
Best Country Song (Songwriter's Award)

1964	"Dang Me," Roger Miller
1965	"King of the Road," Roger Miller
1966	"Almost Persuaded," Billy Sherrill and Glenn Sutton
1967	"Gentle on My Mind," John Hartford
1968	"Little Green Apples," Bobby Russell
1969	"A Boy Named Sue," Shel Silverstein
1970	"My Woman, My Woman, My Wife," Marty Robbins
1971	"Help Me Make It through the Night," Kris Kristofferson
1972	"Kiss an Angel Good Mornin'," Ben Peters
1973	"Behind Closed Doors," Kenny O'Dell
1974	"A Very Special Love Song," Norris Wilson and Billy Sherrill
1975	"(Hey, Won't You Play) Another Somebody Done Somebody Wrong Song," Chips Moman and Larry Butler
1976	"Broken Lady," Larry Gatlin
1977	"Don't It Make My Brown Eyes Blue," Richard Leigh
1978	"The Gambler," Don Schlitz
1979	"You Decorated My Life," Debbie Hupp and Bob Morrison
1980	"On the Road Again," Willie Nelson
1981	"9 to 5," Dolly Parton
1982	"Always on My Mind," Johnny Christopher, Mark James and Wayne Carson
1983	"Stranger in My House," Mike Reid
1984	"City of New Orleans," Steve Goodman
1985	"Highwayman," Jimmy L. Webb
1986	"Grandpa (Tell Me 'bout the Good Old Days)," Jamie O'Hara
1987	"Forever and Ever, Amen," Paul Overstreet and Don Schlitz
1988	"Hold Me," K. T. Oslin
1989	"After All This Time," Rodney Crowell
1990	"Where've You Been?" Jon Vezner and Don Henry
1991	"Love Can Build a Bridge," Naomi Judd, John Jarvis and Paul Overstreet
1992	"I Still Believe in You," Vince Gill and John Barlow Jarvis
1993	"I Still Believe in You," Vince Gill and John Barlow Jarvis
1994	"Passionate Kisses," Lucinda Williams
1995	"I Swear," Gary Baker and Frank J. Myers
1996	"Go Rest High on that Mountain," Vince Gill

Q. Who wrote Glen Campbell's hit "By the Time I Get to Phoenix"?

A. Jimmy Webb.

Q. Texan Al Dexter (Albert Poindexter) wrote what song that became a million-selling record for him and for Bing Crosby?

A. "Pistol Packin' Mama."

Q. Who was known for his closing line, "I'm going to the wagon, these shoes are killin' me"?

A. The Duke of Paducah (Benjamin Francis "Whitey" Ford).

Q. Where was country comedian Archie Campbell born on November 17, 1914?

A. Bulls Gap, Tennessee.

Q. Who wrote the country standard "Country Roads"?

A. John Denver.

Q. Multi-instrumentalist Buddy Emmons was born in what Indiana town on January 27, 1937?

A. Mishawaka.

Q. What song written and recorded by Donna Fargo was the CMA Single of the Year for 1972?

A. "Happiest Girl in the Whole U.S.A."

Q. What 1958 release was Floyd Cramer's first hit record with RCA?

A. "Flip, Flop, and Bop."

———◆———

Q. What 1975 crossover single by Narvel Felts was voted Song of the Year by *Billboard* magazine and Country Song of the Year by *Cashbox* magazine?

A. "Reconsider Baby."

———◆———

Q. Who cowrote "Wasted Days and Wasted Nights" with Freddy Fender?

A. Wayne Duncan.

———◆———

Q. What song, first recorded by the Foggy Mountain Boys in 1949 but released in 1950, was the background music for the car chase in the 1967 motion picture *Bonnie and Clyde*?

A. "Foggy Mountain Breakdown."

———◆———

Q. Who teamed with Patsy and Ed Bruce to compose the theme song for the television series *Bret Maverick*?

A. Glenn Ray.

———◆———

Q. What was the actual name of Tennessee-born fiddler Curly Fox?

A. Arnim LeRoy Fox.

———◆———

Q. Tom T. Hall wrote the lyrics of what song on an air sickness bag on a flight from Atlanta to Nashville?

A. "(Old Dogs, Children, and) Watermelon Wine."

Q. Who was the first writer signed to Dottie West's First Generation music company?

A. Larry Gatlin.

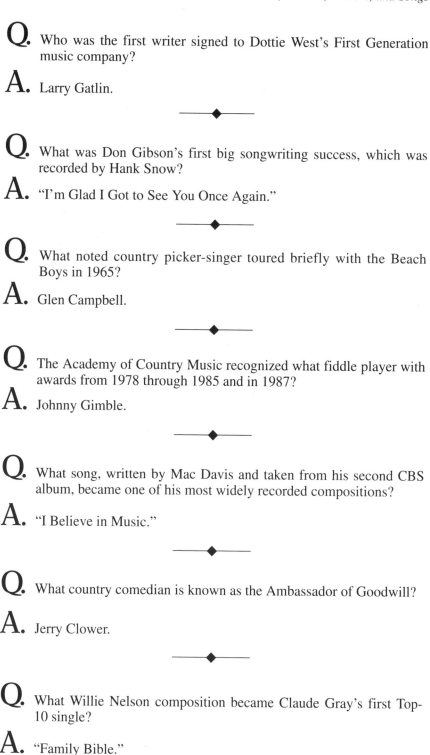

Q. What was Don Gibson's first big songwriting success, which was recorded by Hank Snow?

A. "I'm Glad I Got to See You Once Again."

Q. What noted country picker-singer toured briefly with the Beach Boys in 1965?

A. Glen Campbell.

Q. The Academy of Country Music recognized what fiddle player with awards from 1978 through 1985 and in 1987?

A. Johnny Gimble.

Q. What song, written by Mac Davis and taken from his second CBS album, became one of his most widely recorded compositions?

A. "I Believe in Music."

Q. What country comedian is known as the Ambassador of Goodwill?

A. Jerry Clower.

Q. What Willie Nelson composition became Claude Gray's first Top-10 single?

A. "Family Bible."

Q. Who cowrote Alabama's number-one hit "The Closer You Get"?

A. Mark Gray and James P. Pennington.

———◆———

Q. At what age did Lloyd Green begin taking steel guitar lessons?

A. Seven.

———◆———

Q. Who recorded with RCA Records such comedy routines as "Beeping Sleauty" and "Rindercella"?

A. Archie Campbell.

———◆———

Q. In 1966 what Liz and Casey Anderson composition became Merle Haggard's first number-one hit?

A. "I'm a Lonesome Fugitive."

———◆———

Q. Who composed Jeannie C. Riley's 1968 hit "Harper Valley PTA"?

A. Tom T. Hall.

———◆———

Q. What picker, born in Meherrin, Virginia, won the National Country Music Banjo championship two consecutive years in the late 1940s?

A. Roy Clark.

———◆———

Q. Who wrote and recorded the million sellers "Last Date" and "On the Rebound"?

A. Floyd Cramer.

Q. Who cowrote "Waterloo" with John D. Loudermilk?

A. Marijohn Wilkin.

———◆———

Q. John Sullivan and Rollin Sullivan performed as a comic duo under what stage name from the mid-1940s until 1967?

A. Lonzo and Oscar.

———◆———

Q. What single, written and recorded by Hank Locklin, became a million seller in 1960?

A. "Please Help Me, I'm Falling."

———◆———

Q. Under what pseudonym did Kris Kristofferson compose some of his early songs?

A. Kris Carson.

———◆———

Q. What composition, cowritten by Pee Wee King and Redd Stewart, became the official state song of Tennessee in 1965?

A. "The Tennessee Waltz."

———◆———

Q. Originally released on the Lemon label and later by Decca, what was the title of Jerry Clower's first comedy album?

A. *Jerry Clower from Yazoo City Talkin'.*

———◆———

Q. Who had a double-sided instrumental release in 1959 with "Bonaparte's Retreat" and "The Kissing Tree"?

A. Billy Grammer.

Glen Campbell's music career has included a wide range of styles including country, bluegrass, pop, rock, and gospel. Born in Delight, Arkansas, on April 22, 1936, Glen received his first guitar from his father at age four and by age six had become a reasonably accomplished picker. [BY PERMISSION OF LIBERTY RECORDS]

Q. Who cowrote "Wolverton Mountain" with Claude King?

A. Merle Kilgore.

———◆———

Q. Where was Cajun fiddler Douglas James "Doug" Kershaw born on January 24, 1936?

A. Tiel Ridge, Louisiana.

———◆———

Q. In 1958 what comic single by Simon Crum went to number two on the charts?

A. "Country Music Is Here to Stay."

———◆———

Q. What song cowritten and recorded by John Conlee was a Top-5 hit in 1978?

A. "Rose-Colored Glasses."

———◆———

Q. Who cowrote "Ring of Fire" with Merle Kilgore?

A. June Carter.

———◆———

Q. Who penned Alan Jackson's 1993 megahit single "Chattahoochee"?

A. Jim McBride.

———◆———

Q. What is Don Gibson's most recorded composition?

A. "I Can't Stop Loving You."

The Ryman Auditorium

In the late 1800s, Capt. Thomas Green Ryman owned and operated a fleet of riverboats on the lower Ohio and Cumberland Rivers as well as a saloon on Nashville's Broad Street. He attended a religious revival meeting conducted by evangelist Samuel Porter Jones and was converted on the spot. As a gesture of gratitude for his salvation, Captain Ryman commissioned the architect A. T. Thompson to design a grand revival hall which he would build and name the Union Gospel Tabernacle. The first revival was held in the as-yet-unfinished tabernacle in May 1890. The Confederate Gallery was built in 1897 to accommodate a reunion of Confederate veterans.

Captain Ryman, whose death in 1904 occasioned the renaming of the tabernacle as the Ryman Auditorium, would allow no frivolous activities in the hall during his lifetime. Orators such as William Jennings Bryan and Booker T. Washington spoke in the auditorium, Nashville's symphony and opera guild were housed there, charitable fund-raisers were welcome, and the state gubernatorial conventions were held there in 1892.

Throughout the first half of the twentieth century, many of the world's famous artists and performances appeared at the Ryman: singer Caruso; dancer Isadora Duncan; the operas *Carmen* and *The Barber of Seville;* Helen Hayes, Will Rogers, W. C. Fields, Rudolph Valentino, Charlie Chaplin, Mary Pickford, Douglas Fairbanks, Sarah Bernhardt, Helen Keller and Anne Sullivan Macy, Bob Hope, and Victor Borge were among those who graced the stage.

The Grand Ole Opry began using the Ryman in 1943. The WSM radio barn dance show, which had begun in 1925, had outgrown its earlier homes in the old National Life building, the Hillsboro Theatre, the Dixie Tabernacle, and the War Memorial Building. The show remained in the Ryman Auditorium until moving to the Opryland park in 1974.

It was on the Ryman stage in 1949 that Hank Williams received six encores for "Lovesick Blues" and where Elvis sang in 1954 for his first and only guest appearance on *The Grand Ole Opry*. In 1974 George Morgan sang "Candy Kisses,"

(continued next page)

the last song performed on stage for *The Grand Ole Opry* at Captain Ryman's revered tabernacle. Following an $8.5 million renovation, the Ryman Auditorium reopened in June 1994 to once again host a variety of entertainment events.

Q. What instrument did Waylon Jennings play on Buddy Holly's final tour?

A. Bass guitar.

Q. What banjo picker and guitarist worked with Glen Campbell from 1972 to 1984?

A. Carl Jackson.

Q. How long did it take Jessi Colter to write her 1974 smash hit "I'm Not Lisa"?

A. Five minutes.

Q. Who recorded the country-gospel hit "Wings of a Dove"?

A. Ferlin Husky.

Q. What line of graffiti on a rest-room wall inspired K. T. Oslin's composition "Cornell Crawford"?

A. "I ain't never gonna love nobody but Cornell Crawford."

Q. What was Ferlin Husky's comic alter ego?

A. Simon Crum.

Q. "Pick Me Up on Your Way Down," "Heartaches by the Number," and "I've Got a Tiger by the Tail" are among the works of what noted tunesmith?

A. Harlan Howard.

Q. "Are you ready, Hezzie?" was the opening line of what popular group of comic musicians on *The National Barn Dance*?

A. The Hoosier Hot Shots.

Q. Justin Tubb wrote what number-one hit single for Hawkshaw Hawkins?

A. "Lonesome 7-7203."

Q. The University of Northern Alabama bestowed what honorary degree on George "Goober" Lindsey?

A. Doctor of Humane Letters.

Q. Hank Cochran and Harlan Howard composed what song that was a smash hit for Patsy Cline in 1961?

A. "I Fall to Pieces."

Q. In 1958 guitarist Billy Grammer had what million-selling hit on Monument Records?

A. "Gotta Travel On."

Q. Stuart Hamblen's discovery of a dead man in a dilapidated shack led to his writing what composition?

A. "This Ole House."

Q. Who cowrote the classic "Mountain Dew" with Scotty Wiseman?

A. Bascomb Lamar Lunsford.

Q. The Duke of Paducah and Frankie Marvin formed what comedy team?

A. Ralph and Elmer.

Q. What was the original title of the Don Gibson composition "Oh, Lonesome Me"?

A. "Ole Lonesome Me."

Q. How many different instruments can Cajun fiddler Doug Kershaw play?

A. Twenty-eight.

Q. Harmonica player Charlie McCoy was featured on what 1969 Area Code 615 cut that became the theme song for BBC–TV's *Whistle Test*?

A. "Stone Fox Chase."

Q. What John D. Loudermilk song was a hit for Eddie Cochran in 1957?

A. "Sittin' in the Balcony."

Q. Who's known as "America's dulcimer champion" and has appeared on film with Emmylou Harris and Johnny Cash?

A. David Schnaufer.

Q. Beecher "Pete" Kirby, who plays dobro, banjo, and guitar, is best known by what stage name?

A. Bashful Brother Oswald.

Minnie Pearl and Rod Brasfield (Ray Price visible behind Minnie). A comedy team in the 1940s and 1950s, Minnie remembered Rod (and his brother Boob) from the Brasfields' early performing days traveling with the Bisbee Comedians tent show. Rod and Minnie were the comic stars of the Opry's network portion, The Prince Albert Show, *which starred one of country music's greatest singers and personalities, Clyde Julian "Red" Foley. Their comedy was based on simple, rural humor, and Minnie stated in her autobiography that they played off of one another, never knowing for sure what the other was going to say. Minnie was born Sarah Ophelia Colley in Centerville, Tennessee, about fifty miles west of Nashville. Raised as a lady of culture, she graduated from the elite Ward-Belmont School in Nashville, majoring in speech and drama. She became Minnie Pearl while doing a show in 1936 at Brenlea Mountain in Baileyton, Alabama, where she met a sprightly old mountain woman with a penchant for telling humorous stories. Leon Rodney Brasfield, born in 1910 in Smithville, Mississippi, joined* The Grand Ole Opry *in 1944, four years after Minnie. He died of a heart attack in 1958; she, after a stroke in 1996.* [PHOTO COURTESY OF LES LEVERETT]

Q. Who wrote Ronnie Milsap's 1973 number-one hit single "Pure Love"?

A. Eddie Rabbitt.

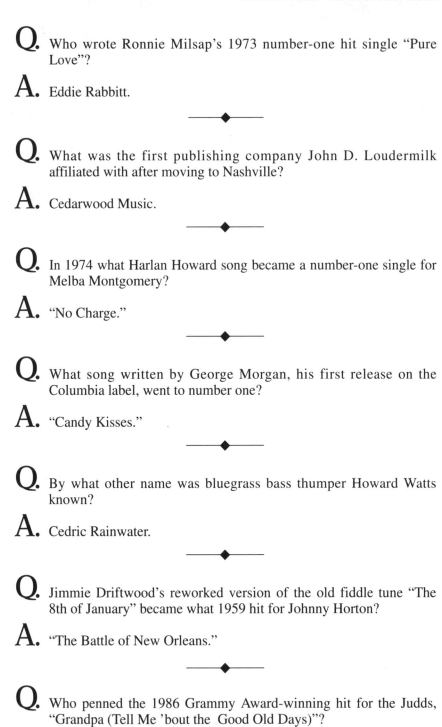

Q. What was the first publishing company John D. Loudermilk affiliated with after moving to Nashville?

A. Cedarwood Music.

Q. In 1974 what Harlan Howard song became a number-one single for Melba Montgomery?

A. "No Charge."

Q. What song written by George Morgan, his first release on the Columbia label, went to number one?

A. "Candy Kisses."

Q. By what other name was bluegrass bass thumper Howard Watts known?

A. Cedric Rainwater.

Q. Jimmie Driftwood's reworked version of the old fiddle tune "The 8th of January" became what 1959 hit for Johnny Horton?

A. "The Battle of New Orleans."

Q. Who penned the 1986 Grammy Award-winning hit for the Judds, "Grandpa (Tell Me 'bout the Good Old Days)"?

A. Jamie O'Hara.

Q. What tune written by Holly Dunn for a Father's Day present became her first Top-10 hit single in 1986?

A. "Daddy's Hands."

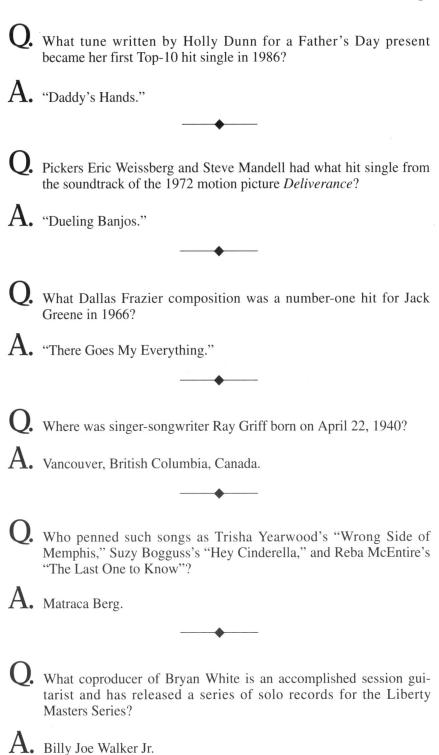

Q. Pickers Eric Weissberg and Steve Mandell had what hit single from the soundtrack of the 1972 motion picture *Deliverance*?

A. "Dueling Banjos."

Q. What Dallas Frazier composition was a number-one hit for Jack Greene in 1966?

A. "There Goes My Everything."

Q. Where was singer-songwriter Ray Griff born on April 22, 1940?

A. Vancouver, British Columbia, Canada.

Q. Who penned such songs as Trisha Yearwood's "Wrong Side of Memphis," Suzy Bogguss's "Hey Cinderella," and Reba McEntire's "The Last One to Know"?

A. Matraca Berg.

Q. What coproducer of Bryan White is an accomplished session guitarist and has released a series of solo records for the Liberty Masters Series?

A. Billy Joe Walker Jr.

Austin City Limits

Austin City Limits is public television's longest-running musical series. It was created by Bill Arhos, station manager at KLRU-TV in Austin, Texas, and filmed on the University of Texas campus. The show was originally conceived to fill the void caused by the antipathy between the "progressive country" or "redneck rock" Austin artists and the Nashville record producers. Some of these artists included Willie Nelson, Jerry Jeff Walker, Michael Martin Murphey, Joe Ely, Johnny Gimble, the Fabulous Thunderbirds, and Stevie Ray Vaughan.

The initial pilot, filmed in October 1974, featured B. W. Stephenson; for the second pilot, produced later the same year, Willie Nelson was approached and offered complete artistic control if he would agree to participate. It was Willie's spontaneous performance that sold the *Austin City Limits* concept, and the show began to air regularly in January 1976.

The purpose of *Austin City Limits*, as expressed by long-time producer Terry Lickona, has been to expose new talent and document the roots and pioneers of American music, including pure country, early rock, blues, and jazz.

Q. Although best known as a harmonica player, Charlie McCoy plays several instruments. How many solo chart records did he have on Monument between 1972 and 1983?

A. Sixteen, topped by "I Started Loving You Again" (number sixteen).

Q. What was pianist-singer Moon Mullican's actual first name?

A. Aubrey.

Q. What Cajun fiddler has appeared in such movies as *Zachariah*, *Medicine Ball Caravan*, and *Days of Heaven*?

A. Doug Kershaw.

Q. What was the cost of the guitar on which Grandpa Jones first learned to play?

A. Seventy-five cents.

———◆———

Q. The song "Good Ol' Boys," written and performed by Waylon Jennings, was the theme song of what 1980s television show?

A. *The Dukes of Hazzard.*

———◆———

Q. What Nashville musician made the "slip-note" piano style internationally famous?

A. Floyd Cramer.

———◆———

Q. What successful 1971 Mickey Newbury work was a medley of Civil War tunes?

A. "An American Trilogy."

———◆———

Q. Inspired by news events, who wrote such songs as "The Death of Floyd Collins" and "The John T. Scopes Trial," which were recorded by Vernon Dalhart?

A. Carson J. Robison.

———◆———

Q. George Nowlan is the actual name of what country trumpeter?

A. Danny Davis.

———◆———

Q. Fiddler-singer Vernon Oxford is a native of what state?

A. Arkansas.

Q. What is the title of the Dorothy Horstman book that contains lyrics and information about how some 360 classic country songs were written?

A. *Sing Your Heart out Country Boy.*

Q. Who wrote the Judds' big hit "Mama, He's Crazy"?

A. Kenny O'Dell.

Q. What album by Chet Atkins and Les Paul won the 1976 Grammy for Best Country Instrumental Performance in 1977?

A. *Chester & Lester.*

Q. What composition gave Tammy Wynette her first hit single?

A. "Apartment No. 9."

Q. "Howdy, I'm just so proud to be here" was the famous opening line of what comic performer?

A. Minnie Pearl.

Q. The Statler Brothers' 1965 hit "Flowers on the Wall" was written by what member of their group?

A. Lew De Witt.

Q. What is the actual surname of Georgia-born singer-comedian Ray Stevens?

A. Ragsdale.

Q. What Texan cowrote Buck Owens's 1966 hit "Waitin' in Your Welfare Line" with Don Rich and Buck Owens?

A. Nat Stuckey.

———◆———

Q. What music pioneer claimed to be the first steel guitar player in country music?

A. John James Rimbert "Jimmie" Tarlton.

———◆———

Q. During the late 1940s, what composer wrote such songs as "I Love You So Much, It Hurts," "Slippin' Around," and "I'll Never Slip Around Again"?

A. Floyd Tillman.

———◆———

Q. Before he cowrote "I Swear" and launched a career with Frank Myers, Gary Baker belonged to what groups?

A. LeBlanc and Carr, and the Shooters.

———◆———

Q. Joy White's "True Confessions" chart single was cowritten with what popular entertainer?

A. Marty Stuart.

———◆———

Q. Where did the King of Pumpin' Piano, Moon Mullican, die from a heart attack on January 1, 1967?

A. Beaumont, Texas.

———◆———

Q. What two Ray Pennington compositions were hits for Kenny Price in 1966?

A. "Walking on New Grass" and "Happy Tracks."

Q. For whom did Jeanne Pruett's husband, Jack, play lead guitar for almost fourteen years?

A. Marty Robbins.

Q. As a staff writer at Hill and Range Music Publishing, Eddie Rabbitt wrote what 1970 Elvis Presley hit?

A. "Kentucky Rain."

Q. What instrument did Willie Nelson play with Ray Price's band?

A. Bass guitar.

Q. Taken from an interview over a Macon, Georgia, radio station, what became Junior Samples's first comic release with Chart Records in 1967?

A. "The World's Biggest Whopper."

Q. Who wrote most of the songs on Waylon Jennings's 1973 album *Honky-Tonk Heroes*?

A. Billy Joe Shaver.

Q. Who was the first country musician to be recorded in the field (by Ralph Peer in Atlanta, Georgia, in June 1923)?

A. Fiddlin' John Carson.

Q. What two songs written by Johnny Cash were on his first release by Sun Records?

A. "Hey, Porter" and "Cry! Cry! Cry!"

CMA Single of the Year

1967   "There Goes My Everything"/Jack Greene/Decca
1968   "Harper Valley P.T.A."/Jeannie C. Riley/Plantation
1969   "A Boy Named Sue"/Johnny Cash/Columbia
1970   "Okie from Muskogee"/Merle Haggard/Capitol
1971   "Help Me Make It through the Night"/Sammi Smith/
        Mega
1972   "The Happiest Girl in the Whole U.S.A."/Donna
        Fargo/Dot
1973   "Behind Closed Doors"/Charlie Rich/Epic
1974   "Country Bumpkin"/Cal Smith/MCA
1975   "Before the Next Teardrop Falls"/Freddy Fender/
        ABC-Dot
1976   "Good Hearted Woman"/Waylon Jennings and Willie
        Nelson/RCA
1977   "Lucille"/Kenny Rogers/United Artists
1978   "Heaven's Just a Sin Away"/The Kendalls/Ovation
1979   "The Devil Went down to Georgia"/Charlie Daniels
        Band/Epic
1980   "He Stopped Loving Her Today"/George Jones/Epic
1981   "Elvira"/Oak Ridge Boys/MCA
1982   "Always on My Mind"/Willie Nelson/Columbia
1983   "Swingin'"/John Anderson/Warner Bros.
1984   "A Little Good News"/Anne Murray/Capitol
1985   "Why Not Me"/the Judds/RCA
1986   "Bop"/Dan Seals/EMI-America
1987   "Forever and Ever, Amen"/Randy Travis/Warner Bros.
1988   "Eighteen Wheels and a Dozen Roses"/Kathy
        Mattea/PolyGram
1989   "I'm No Stranger to the Rain"/Keith Whitley/RCA
1990   "When I Call Your Name"/Vince Gill/MCA
1991   "Friends in Low Places"/Garth Brooks/Capitol
        Nashville
1992   "Achy Breaky Heart"/Billy Ray Cyrus/Mercury
1993   "Chattahoochee"/Alan Jackson/Arista
1994   "I Swear"/John Michael Montgomery/Atlantic
1995   "When You Say Nothing at All"/Alison Krauss and
        Union Station/BNA

Q. What country comic started his showbiz career as a teenager selling peanuts and popcorn with the J. G. O'Brian Stock Company?

A. Rod Brasfield.

Q. Jim Glaser and Jimmy Payne wrote what song that was a million seller for Gary Puckett and the Union Gap?

A. "Woman, Woman."

Q. In 1961 what was Ray Stevens's first novelty tune to make the charts?

A. "Jeremiah Peabody's Polyunsaturated Quick Dissolving Fast Acting, Pleasant Tasting, Green and Purple Pills."

Q. What Tennessee community did the character Minnie Pearl claim as her hometown?

A. Grinder's Switch.

Q. Released in 1941 what song written by Ernest Tubb was his first million-selling record?

A. "Walking the Floor over You."

Q. What Mel Tillis composition became a hit for Kenny Rogers in 1969?

A. "Ruby, Don't Take Your Love to Town."

Q. What Johnny Russell composition was a 1963 chart-topper for Buck Owens and was later recorded by the Beatles?

A. "Act Naturally."

CMA Album of the Year

1967   *There Goes My Everything*/Jack Greene/Decca
1968   *Johnny Cash at Folsom Prison*/Johnny Cash/Columbia
1969   *Johnny Cash at San Quentin Prison*/Johnny Cash/
       Columbia
1970   *Okie from Muskogee*/Merle Haggard/Capitol
1971   *I Won't Mention It Again*/Ray Price/Columbia
1972   *Let Me Tell You about a Song*/Merle Haggard/Capitol
1973   *Behind Closed Doors*/Charlie Rich/Epic
1974   *A Very Special Love Song*/Charlie Rich/Epic
1975   *A Legend in My Time*/Ronnie Milsap/RCA
1976   *Wanted—The Outlaws*/Waylon Jennings, Willie
       Nelson, Tompall Glaser, Jessi Colter/RCA
1977   *Ronnie Milsap Live*/Ronnie Milsap/RCA
1978   *It Was Almost like a Song*/Ronnie Milsap/RCA
1979   *The Gambler*/Kenny Rogers/United Artists
1980   *Coal Miner's Daughter*/Original Motion Picture
       Soundtrack/MCA
1981   *I Believe in You*/Don Williams/MCA
1982   *Always on My Mind*/Willie Nelson/Columbia
1983   *The Closer You Get*/Alabama/RCA
1984   *A Little Good News*/Anne Murray/Capitol
1985   *Does Fort Worth Ever Cross Your Mind?*/George
       Strait/ MCA
1986   *Lost in the Fifties Tonight*/Ronnie Milsap/RCA
1987   *Always and Forever*/Randy Travis/Warner Bros.
1988   *Born to Boogie*/Hank Williams Jr./Warner Bros.
1989   *Will the Circle Be Unbroken, Vol. II*/Nitty Gritty Dirt
       Band/Universal
1990   *Pickin' on Nashville*/Kentucky HeadHunters/Mercury
1991   *No Fences*/Garth Brooks/Capitol Nashville
1992   *Ropin' the Wind*/Garth Brooks/Liberty
1993   *I Still Believe in You*/Vince Gill/MCA
1994   *Common Thread: The Songs of the Eagles*/John
       Anderson, Clint Black, Suzy Bogguss, Brooks &
       Dunn, Billy Dean, Diamond Rio, Vince Gill, Alan
       Jackson, Little Texas, Lorrie Morgan, Travis Tritt,
       Tanya Tucker, Trisha Yearwood/ Giant Records
1995   *When Fallen Angels Fly*/Patty Loveless/Epic Records

Q. Becky Hobbs penned what song that she says was inspired by a personal angelic encounter?

A. "Angels among Us."

Q. What was the only single from Garth Brooks's first album for Capitol Records, *Garth Brooks,* that he did not write or cowrite?

A. "The Dance."

Q. What sixteen-year-old picker joined the Light Crust Doughboys in 1933?

A. Leon McAuliffe.

Q. What Boudleaux Bryant composition was a major career breakthrough for Bob Luman in 1960?

A. "Let's Think about Living."

Q. What was the telephone number for Junior Samples's used-car lot on *Hee Haw*?

A. BR–549.

Q. Beginning in 1950 what song, written and recorded by Hank Snow, stayed on the charts for over forty weeks?

A. "I'm Moving On."

Q. What composition, cowritten by Gary Stewart and Bill Eldridge, was a hit for Nat Stuckey in 1969?

A. "Sweet Thang and Cisco."

Perhaps the most imitated pianist in popular music, Floyd Cramer's "slip-note" style can be heard on dozens of country hits of the 1950s, 1960s, and 1970s. In addition he fashioned numerous pop and country hits as a solo act, most notably "Last Date," "On the Rebound," and "San Antonio Rose." Beginning in 1957 and continuing for a quarter-century, Cramer released at least one album a year of instrumental piano music. As a protégé of Chet Atkins, Cramer was a key cog in the development of the "Nashville sound." His signature song, "Last Date," with lyrics added, became a hit twice more in versions by Conway Twitty and Emmylou Harris in the 1970s and 1980s. [PHOTO PROVIDED BY RCA RECORDS]

Q. What comedian-musician and his wife were murdered by intruders as they returned home from a *Grand Ole Opry* performance on November 19, 1973?

A. Stringbean and his wife, Estelle.

Q. What member of the Sons of the Pioneers composed "Tumbling Tumbleweeds" and "Cool Water"?

A. Bob Nolan (Robert Clarence Nobles).

Q. What long-time member and manager of the Sons of the Pioneers penned "Cigareetes, Whisky, and Wild Women," "Careless Kisses," and "Room Full of Roses"?

A. Tim Spencer.

Q. What song composed and recorded by T. Texas Tyler in 1948 also provided a hit for Wink Martindale and for Tex Ritter?

A. "Deck of Cards."

Q. Who cowrote the 1956 hit "The Auctioneer" with Leroy Van Dyke?

A. Buddy Black.

Q. Who was the first performer to play the electric banjo on Porter Wagoner's television show?

A. Buck Trent.

Q. With whom did Merle Haggard cowrite his biggest career hit single "Okie from Muskogee"?

A. Roy Burris.

Q. What journalist, artist, librarian, author, and TV writer and personality is unquestionably the leading Nashville media figure covering country music?

A. Robert K. Oermann.

Q. In what year did Ray Stevens have his hit "Ahab the Arab"?

A. 1962.

Q. What drummer was Dottie West's last husband?

A. Bryon Metcalf.

Q. Billy Edd Wheeler wrote what song that made the Top 10 in the pop charts for the Kingston Trio in 1963?

A. "The Reverend Mr. Black."

Q. What is saxophonist Boots Randolph's real name?

A. Homer Louis Randolph III.

Q. Who cowrote "Jackson," the Johnny Cash and June Carter hit, and "Coward of the County," Kenny Rogers's multimillion seller?

A. Billy Edd Wheeler.

Q. Who cowrote with Fred Rose, Gene Autry's big hit "Back in the Saddle Again"?

A. Ray Whitley.

Q. Dennis Linde, one of country's top writers of the 1990s, penned what Elvis Presley smash?

A. "Burning Love."

Q. Of her many compositions, which is Dolly Parton's personal favorite?

A. "Coat of Many Colors."

The Country Music Hall of Fame and Museum

The largest museum devoted to a single form of popular music, the Country Music Hall of Fame and Museum was opened in April 1967. The Country Music Association (CMA), along with country music industry leaders such as Tex Ritter and producer Owen Bradley, raised the initial $750,000 needed for the building's construction. The Country Music Foundation (CMF), a nonprofit, educational organization dedicated to the preservation of country music history, administers the museum and operates a media center and library in the building's basement.

Hall of Fame Members

Year of
Induction

1961	Jimmie Rodgers, Fred Rose, Hank Williams
1962	Roy Acuff
1963	Elections held, but no candidate had enough votes
1964	Tex Ritter
1965	Ernest Tubb
1966	James R. "Jim" Denny, George D. Hay, Uncle Dave Macon, Eddy Arnold
1967	Red Foley, J. L. "Joe" Frank, Jim Reeves, Stephen H. Sholes
1968	Bob Wills
1969	Gene Autry
1970	Original Carter Family (A. P. Carter, Maybelle Carter, Sara Carter), Bill Monroe
1971	Arthur Edward "Art" Satherley
1972	Jimmie Davis
1973	Patsy Cline, Chet Atkins
1974	Owen Bradley, Frank "Pee Wee" King
1975	Minnie Pearl
1976	Paul Cohen, Kitty Wells
1977	Merle Travis
1978	Louis Marshall "Grandpa" Jones
1979	Hubert Long, Hank Snow
1980	Connie B. Gay, Original Sons of the Pioneers (Leonard Slye [Roy Rogers], Tim Spencer, Bob Nolan, Hugh Farr, Karl Farr, Lloyd Perryman), Johnny Cash
1981	Vernon Dalhart, Grant Turner
1982	Lefty Frizzell, Marty Robbins, Roy Horton
1983	Little Jimmy Dickens
1984	Ralph Peer, Floyd Tillman
1985	Lester Flatt and Earl Scruggs
1986	Wesley Rose, the Duke of Paducah
1987	Rod Brasfield
1988	Roy Rogers, Loretta Lynn
1989	Jack Stapp, Hank Thompson, Cliffie Stone
1990	Tennessee Ernie Ford
1991	Boudleaux and Felice Bryant
1992	George Jones, Frances Preston
1993	Willie Nelson
1994	Merle Haggard
1995	Jo Walker-Meador

Q. Who cowrote "You and I" for Eddie Rabbitt and Crystal Gayle, "I've Got Mexico" for Eddy Raven, and was a band member for Raven and Marie Osmond?

A. Frank Myers.

———◆———

Q. Who wrote Hank Williams's hit "Half as Much"?

A. Curly Williams.

———◆———

Q. What song written by Johnny Cash was based on the flooding of the Mississippi River in 1937?

A. "Five Feet High and Rising."

———◆———

Q. First released as an instrumental in 1938, what song written by Bob Wills became a million seller for him in 1940 and later a million seller for Bing Crosby?

A. "San Antonio Rose."

———◆———

Q. Early in his association with *The Grand Ole Opry* what country comic was known as the Hohenwald Flash?

A. Rod Brasfield.

———◆———

Q. In 1944 what *Grand Ole Opry* star was honored by having Tennessee Walking Horse Number 442588 from Harlinsdale Farm in Franklin, Tennessee, named for her?

A. Minnie Pearl.

———◆———

Q. What song written by Kenny O'Dell became a hit single for Charlie Rich in 1973?

A. "Behind Closed Doors."

Country comic George "Goober" Lindsey was a halfback on the Florence State (now University of North Alabama) football team and gave up a coaching career to go into show business. Goober became a nationally recognized character on The Andy Griffith Show *and* Mayberry R.F.D. *Later Goober became a regular cast member of* Hee Haw. [PHOTO COURTESY OF DONNA JACKSON]

Q. What member of Roy Acuff's show during the mid-1940s was the only woman picking five-string banjo on network radio?

A. Rachel Watson.

———◆———

Q. Dennis Robbins cowrote what song for Shenandoah?

A. "The Church on the Cumberland Road."

———◆———

Q. Still active today, who played fiddle for Bob Wills in the early 1950s and toured with Willie Nelson for many years?

A. Johnny Gimble, of Tyler, Texas. He also plays mandolin and banjo.

———◆———

Q. What 1969 hit did Merle Haggard compose in his tour bus near Tucson, Arizona?

A. "Workin' Man Blues."

Q. What character became Sheb Wooley's comic alter ego?

A. Ben Colder.

Q. What Canadian singer-songwriter wrote George Hamilton IV's 1971 hit "Countryfied"?

A. Dick Damron.

Q. What *Grand Ole Opry* comic of the 1930s and 1940s was known for his singing news routine?

A. Lazy Jim Day.

Q. Who reworked the old fiddle tune "Bonaparte's Retreat" to make it a popular song of the 1950s?

A. Redd Stewart.

Q. What member of the Country Music Hall of Fame had a father who performed as Herman the Hermit?

A. Cliffie Stone.

Q. Who cowrote with Vince Gill the 1992 CMA Song of the Year "Look at Us"?

A. Max D. Barnes.

Q. What song that he wrote did Marty Brown introduce at the 1992 Kentucky Derby?

A. "Kentucky Skies."

Q. The amphibious naval vessel USS *LCT 514* was renamed in honor of what country comic on April 24, 1945?

A. Minnie Pearl.

Q. On November 28, 1925, what octogenarian inaugurated *The WSM Barn Dance* by playing his "blue ribbon" fiddle?

A. Uncle Jimmy Thompson.

Q. Guitarist Billy Grammer had what million-seller hit in 1958?

A. "Gotta Travel On."

Q. Who wrote the Oak Ridge Boys' hit "Bobbie Sue"?

A. Wood Newton, Dan Tyler, and Adele Tyler.

Q. What thirteen-year-old performer started playing piano on *The WSM Barn Dance* with her father's string band, the Possum Hunters?

A. Alcyone Bates.

Q. Early in his career Cowboy Copas performed with what native American fiddler?

A. Natchee.

Q. Who became the best-known dobro player in Nashville during the 1980s and 1990s?

A. Jerry "Flux" Douglas.

Q. Bob Millard has written songs for Kathy Mattea and numerous books about country music. Name the two acts whose lives Millard chronicled in his 1980s unauthorized biographies.

A. Amy Grant, and the Judds.

———◆———

Q. Ricky Skaggs had a 1982 hit of what Flatt and Scruggs 1960 hit?

A. "Crying My Heart Out over You."

———◆———

Q. What fiddler associated with Buck Owens's show for many years was the winner of the National Ladies Fiddling championship in 1973 and 1974?

A. Jana Jae.

———◆———

Q. Who wrote the Billy Ray Cyrus megahit "Achy Breaky Heart"?

A. Don VonTress.

———◆———

Q. What blind piano player was selected by the CMA in 1976 as Instrumentalist of the Year?

A. Hargus "Pig" Robbins.

———◆———

Q. Who cowrote the Holly Dunn hit "There Goes My Heart Again"?

A. Joe Diffie, Lonnie Wilson, and Wayne Perry.

———◆———

Q. Who worked simultaneously as Kitty Wells's steelman and Johnny and Jack's dobro player?

A. Shot Jackson.

(l to r) front row: Two of the greatest guitar designers and innovators of the twentieth century, Leo Fender, founder of Fender Guitars, and Shot Jackson of Sho-Bud pedal steel guitar fame. Back row: Texas Troubadour Ernest Tubb; the Queen of Country Music, Kitty Wells, with husband Johnny Wright; Jack Anglin; Forrest White, an assistant of Leo Fender; and guitarist Billy Byrd. [PHOTO COURTESY OF DONNA JACKSON]

Q. Who cowrote "It Only Hurts When I Cry" with Roger Miller?

A. Dwight Yoakam.

◆

Q. Banjo picker Buck Trent is a native of what South Carolina city?

A. Spartanburg.

Q. What composer of such hits as "Honey," "Little Green Apples," and "The Night the Lights Went Out in Georgia" was chosen Songwriter of the Year in 1968 by the Nashville Songwriters Association?

A. Bobby Russell.

------◆------

Q. Who is said to have been the first person to use an autoharp in a country recording?

A. Ernest V. "Pop" Stoneman.

------◆------

Q. By what other stage name was banjo picker Stringbean known?

A. The Kentucky Wonder.

------◆------

Q. Actor-singer-songwriter Tom Wopat wrote what successful Earl Thomas Conley single?

A. "Shadow of a Doubt."

Country Song Round-up **Magazine**

Inaugural issue: July/August 1949
Articles on Roy Acuff, Rosalie Allen, Eddy Arnold, *The National Barn Dance*, Judy Canova, Cowboy Copas, Andy Parker and the Plainsmen, Roy Rogers, Jimmy Wakely, Tex Williams
Other features and columns: questions and answers, record reviews, "Where the [Radio] Acts Are Playing," "West Coast Corral"
Lyrics to: "Born to Lose," I Love You So Much It Hurts," "Tennessee Waltz," "Riders in the Sky," "Pan American," "Move It on Over," "Texarkana Baby," "I Don't Care If Tomorrow Never Comes," "Blue Eyes Cryin' in the Rain," "I'm Thinking Tonight of My Blue Eyes," and more
Single copy: 25¢; yearly subscription: $1.50

Q. What two songwriters collaborated on Trisha Yearwood's hit "Walk Away, Joe"?

A. Vince Melamed and Greg Barnhill.

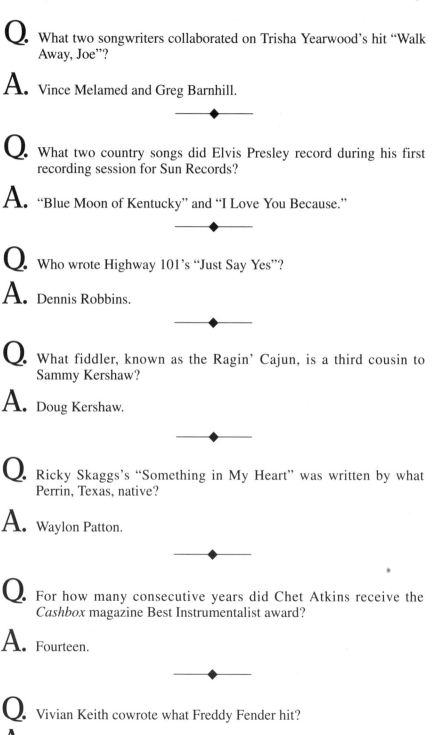

Q. What two country songs did Elvis Presley record during his first recording session for Sun Records?

A. "Blue Moon of Kentucky" and "I Love You Because."

Q. Who wrote Highway 101's "Just Say Yes"?

A. Dennis Robbins.

Q. What fiddler, known as the Ragin' Cajun, is a third cousin to Sammy Kershaw?

A. Doug Kershaw.

Q. Ricky Skaggs's "Something in My Heart" was written by what Perrin, Texas, native?

A. Waylon Patton.

Q. For how many consecutive years did Chet Atkins receive the *Cashbox* magazine Best Instrumentalist award?

A. Fourteen.

Q. Vivian Keith cowrote what Freddy Fender hit?

A. "Before the Next Teardrop Falls."

Q. What Louisiana singer-songwriter wrote "Poke Salad Annie," "For Ol' Times Sake," and "Rainy Night in Georgia"?

A. Tony Joe White.

———◆———

Q. Mark Chesnutt's second hit, "Brother Jukebox," was composed by what songwriter?

A. Paul Craft.

———◆———

Q. What British-born guitarist became known to country fans through session work and his live dates in bands with the Everly Brothers, Linda Ronstadt, and Eric Clapton?

A. Albert Lee.

———◆———

Q. Who co-composed Ronnie Milsap's hits "Stranger in the House" and "Lost in the Fifties Tonight"?

A. Mike Reid.

———◆———

Q. Which of his songs did Hank Williams Jr. rewrite, turning it into "Monday Night Football Boogie," the theme song of ABC-TV's *Monday Night Football*?

A. "All My Rowdy Friends (Are Coming Over Tonight)."

———◆———

Q. What female comic and banjo picker was for many years a regular on *Hee Haw*?

A. Roni Stoneman.

———◆———

Q. In 1969 what Shel Silverstein song became Johnny Cash's biggest crossover into the pop charts?

A. "A Boy Named Sue."

WSM PHOTO
By Les Leverett

Banjo player and comedian David "Stringbean" Akeman and his wife, Estelle, were murdered by intruders on November 10, 1973, as they returned home to their small farmhouse after an Opry performance. Stringbean was born in 1916 in Anneville, Kentucky, and grew up on a farm with his four brothers and three sisters. His father, also an expert banjo player, gave his son his first banjo when he was fourteen, and David soon began entertaining at local square dances and other social events. A radio announcer with station WLAP in Lexington, Kentucky, forgot David's name as he was about to introduce him over the air, and said, "Come here, stringbean, and play us a tune" — and the nickname stuck. A Grand Ole Opry *member since 1942, Stringbean's standard opening line was, "How sweet it is!"* [PHOTO COURTESY OF LES LEVERETT]

Q. What longtime *Grand Ole Opry* harmonica player performed under the pseudonym of Miller Bill?

A. Herman Crook.

———◆———

Q. A chance meeting with an ex-girlfriend led Bill Anderson to compose what song that became a hit single for him in 1963?

A. "Still."

———◆———

Q. What was the stage name of David Akeman?

A. Stringbean.

———◆———

Q. What was the original title of "Statue of a Fool," which was a hit single for Jack Greene in 1969?

A. "Name It after Me."

———◆———

Q. What Japanese fiddler is headquartered in Branson, Missouri?

A. Shoji Tabuchi.

———◆———

Q. The Geezinslaw Brothers had what hit country jukebox song in 1992?

A. "Help, I'm White and I Can't Get Down."

———◆———

Q. A Russian version of what Conway Twitty tune was played on the historic American-Russian cooperative space mission, Apollo-Soyuz, in 1975?

A. "Hello Darlin'" (*"Privet Radost"*).

Q. Who is Shotgun Red's protégé?

A. Steve Hall.

———◆———

Q. What 1970 hit for Johnny Cash was delivered by songwriter Kris Kristofferson by landing a helicopter on Cash's lawn one Sunday morning?

A. "Sunday Morning Coming Down."

———◆———

Q. Whom has Vince Gill called the "best musician on the planet"?

A. Mark O'Connor.

———◆———

Q. What 1971 Charley Pride single was written by Johnny Duncan following a program at the Tri-State Fair in Amarillo, Texas?

A. "I'd Rather Love You."

———◆———

Q. Banjo picker Mike Snider of TNN, *Hee Haw*, and *Grand Ole Opry* fame hails from what Tennessee town?

A. Gleason.

———◆———

Q. What Freddie Hart composition was the first country song to go number one that contained the term *sexy*?

A. "Easy Loving."

———◆———

Q. What songwriter and performer is known as the Storyteller?

A. Tom T. Hall.

***Music City News* Magazine**

Inaugural issue: July 1963.
Lead story: Twelve-page photo/journalistic story of Audrey
   Williams's movie *Country Music on Broadway.*
Front page: photo of Elvis advertising a story in the next issue
Other features:
- Articles about Stonewall Jackson, Kitty Wells, Bobby
   Helms
- Surf music feature, questions and answers, stars' tour
   schedules
- Columns: "Know Your Opry Stars," "News and Views
   of the Fans," "What Is, Was, and Will Be"

Number-one single: "We Must Have Been Out of Our Minds"
   —George Jones and Tammy Wynette
Single-copy cost: 35¢; yearly subscription: $3.00   (George
   Jones was one of the first ten people to subscribe.)

Q. What Doug Kershaw song was broadcast to Earth from the 1969
Apollo 12 space mission?

A. "Louisiana Man."

Q. Fiddler-singer Clinton Gregory is a native of what Virginia town?

A. Martinsville.

Q. What Mississippian wrote such hit songs as "I've Never Picked
Cotton," "I've Got Stripes," and "500 Miles Away from Home"?

A. Charlie Williams III.

Q. Sonny James's country and pop hit "Running Bear" was written by
what rock and roll pioneer?

A. The Big Bopper (J. P. Richardson).

Q. What is the actual name of country comic Speck Rhodes?

A. Gilbert Ray Rhodes.

Q. Who wrote and recorded the hit single "Here's a Quarter (Call Someone Who Cares)"?

A. Travis Tritt.

Q. What two performers make up the comedy team known as the Indian and the White Man?

A. Bruce Williams and Terry Ree.

Q. Ed and Patsy Bruce composed what song that went to number one for Waylon Jennings and Willie Nelson in 1978?

A. "Mammas, Don't Let Your Babies Grow Up to Be Cowboys."

Q. How long did it take Boudleaux and Felice Bryant to compose their classic "Rocky Top"?

A. Ten minutes.

Q. What were the actual names of the 1930s *Grand Ole Opry* comedy duo of Sarie and Sallie?

A. Edna Wilson and Margaret Waters.

Q. How did Grady Martin create his "fuzz-tone" guitar sound that so distinguishes the Marty Robbins hit "Don't Worry 'bout Me"?

A. He used an amplifier.

Q. What singer-songwriter had his first Top-10 hit in 1959 with the recording of his "Am I That Easy to Forget?"

A. Carl Belew.

———◆———

Q. What was the actual name of Cousin Jody, who was known for his comic pantomime and steel guitar work?

A. James Clell Summey.

———◆———

Q. In September 1962 Rex Allen's Mercury recording of what song broke into the Top-20 chart?

A. "Don't Go Near the Indians."

———◆———

Q. What singer-songwriter was born Elizabeth Jane Haaby on March 13, 1930, at Rosean, Minnesota?

A. Liz Anderson.

———◆———

Q. Whom did Bill Monroe immortalize in his classic bluegrass composition "Uncle Pen"?

A. Pendleton Vandiver.

———◆———

Q. Born near Luttrell, Tennessee, on June 20, 1924, what is Chet Atkins's full name?

A. Chester Burton Atkins.

———◆———

Q. What singer-songwriter is the only entertainer to be honored with five stars on the Walk of Fame in Hollywood, California?

A. Gene Autry.

5

More of the Industry

Q. Who was the first country artist to appear on a broadcast via satellite?

A. Bill Anderson.

————◆————

Q. From what city did the *Eddy Arnold Time* syndicated television show originate from 1954 to 1956?

A. Springfield, Missouri.

————◆————

Q. Where is Alabama's annual June Jam held?

A. Fort Payne.

————◆————

Q. In what 1980 movie did Dolly Parton costar with Jane Fonda and Lily Tomlin?

A. *9 to 5.*

————◆————

Q. What long-time member of Chicago's *National Barn Dance* served almost two decades as the mayor of Schaumburg, Illinois?

A. Bob Atcher.

Q. What is the name of Vince Gill's music publishing company?

A. Benefit Music.

───────◆───────

Q. The name of the Sho-Bud steel guitar company was created from the names of what cofounders?

A. <u>Sho</u>t Jackson and <u>Bud</u>dy Emmons.

───────◆───────

Q. Who sang the Oscar-winning theme song "High Noon" ("Do Not Forsake Me, Oh My Darlin'") for the 1952 movie with the same title?

A. Tex Ritter.

───────◆───────

Q. On what country program did Elvis Presley make his television debut in March 1955?

A. *The Louisiana Hayride.*

───────◆───────

Q. What positions did Charley Pride play with the Memphis Red Sox in the mid-1950s?

A. Pitcher and outfield.

───────◆───────

Q. In 1963 Jim Reeves starred in what movie filmed in South Africa?

A. *Kimberly Jim.*

───────◆───────

Q. Who cohosted *Town Hall Party* with Johnny Bond from 1953 to 1960?

A. Tex Ritter.

Shreveport's Louisiana Hayride *served as a springboard for the careers of many performers. (l to r) Program director Horace Logan, announcer Ed Hamilton, and Elvis Presley backstage at the* Louisiana Hayride. *Elvis first appeared on the show October 16, 1954, with his final appearance being December 16, 1956.* [PHOTO COURTESY OF SKIP JACKSON]

Q. What country singer-yodeler was the voice of one of the dwarfs in Walt Disney's classic *Snow White and the Seven Dwarfs*?

A. Zeke Clements.

◆

Q. What country star has appeared in such motion pictures as *Frank and Jesse, At Risk, Dead Man's Revenge, Maverick,* and *The Legend of O.B. Taggarat*?

A. Randy Travis.

CMA Entertainer of the Year

1967	Eddy Arnold	1982	Alabama
1968	Glen Campbell	1983	Alabama
1969	Johnny Cash	1984	Alabama
1970	Merle Haggard	1985	Ricky Skaggs
1971	Charley Pride	1986	Reba McEntire
1972	Loretta Lynn	1987	Hank Williams Jr.
1973	Roy Clark	1988	Hank Williams Jr.
1974	Charlie Rich	1989	George Strait
1975	John Denver	1990	George Strait
1976	Mel Tillis	1991	Garth Brooks
1977	Ronnie Milsap	1992	Garth Brooks
1978	Dolly Parton	1993	Vince Gill
1979	Willie Nelson	1994	Vince Gill
1980	Barbara Mandrell	1995	Alan Jackson
1981	Barbara Mandrell		

Q. What singer-songwriter-actor wrote books about Gene Autry and Tex Ritter and his autobiography, *Reflections*?

A. Johnny Bond.

◆

Q. When did *The Glen Campbell Goodtime Hour* air on television?

A. From January 29, 1969, to June 13, 1972.

◆

Q. What is the name of Reba McEntire's charter airplane company?

A. Starstruck Aviation.

◆

Q. What TNN program was hosted by Riders in the Sky from 1985 to 1988?

A. *Tumbleweed Theater.*

Q. What do the initials *SOR* stand for in the recording company founded in Nashville in 1984?

A. Step One Records.

———◆———

Q. What is the nickname of Aaron Tippin's old Toyota Corolla that inspired his hit "There Ain't Nothin' Wrong with the Radio"?

A. Daisy.

———◆———

Q. In October 1993 what new program replaced Ralph Emery's long-running *Nashville Now* on TNN?

A. *Music City Tonight.*

———◆———

Q. When *Music City News* first published in 1963, what was its annual subscription rate?

A. Three dollars.

———◆———

Q. Country music personality Jack Clement produced what horror film?

A. *Dear Dead Delilah.*

———◆———

Q. In 1966 who recorded a program of old-time bluegrass music for broadcast on Radio Moscow?

A. Bill Clifton.

———◆———

Q. What syndicated television show that first aired in 1976 was cohosted by Jerry Clower?

A. *Nashville on the Road.*

Branson, Missouri

In the early 1880s, Reuben Branson chose the point where merchants and traders regularly crossed southern Missouri's White River to build his general store and post office. The city took his name and now rivals Nashville, Tennessee, for country music tourism. Yet it was Branson's natural beauty that initially lured visitors to the vicinity more than one-half century before the first music theaters were ever built.

With the completion of a railroad line through Branson in the early 1900s, campgrounds and hotels sprang up to accommodate travelers and fishermen. However, it was the publication of Harold Bell Wright's 1907 novel set in Branson, *The Shepherd of the Hills,* that firmly established Branson as a tourist attraction. Written while Wright was camping at nearby Inspiration Point, the book was the fourth most widely published book in history.

In 1946 the Herschend family purchased the land containing Marvel Cave and began to offer tours of this natural wonder. Soon gift shops and restaurants appeared. In 1960 the Herschends opened Silver Dollar City, a replica of an Ozark pioneer settlement with rides, crafts, food, and shows. In that same year the outdoor passion play *The Shepherd of the Hills,* based on the novel, debuted on the site where Harold Wright had camped and drafted his historical work. The new Table Rock Dam on the White River eventually formed Table Rock Lake and Lake Taneycomo, greatly increasing Branson's appeal as an all-around vacation spot.

During this time, the Mabe Brothers, who adopted the name the Baldknobbers (an Ozark vigilante group from the Civil War era), and the Presley Family, all veterans of Springfield, Missouri, radio, began to informally entertain the growing crowds at the campgrounds and other Branson gathering places. In 1967 the Presleys opened the first permanent theater on Branson's West Highway 76 strip. Their *Mountain Music Jubilee* continues to be a popular attraction today, as does the Baldknobbers' Hillbilly Jamboree Theatre, which was built the following year. By 1975, the Foggy River Boys and the Plummer family had also established theaters along West

(continued next page)

[PHOTO COURTESY OF BRANSON LAKES AREA CHAMBER OF COMMERCE]

76, but it would not be until the early 1980s that the real boom would begin.

In 1983 Roy Clark opened his Celebrity Dinner Theatre and began to book big-name country music entertainers. The Sons of the Pioneers, Boxcar Willie, Cristy Lane, Danny Davis and the Nashville Brass, and Japanese violinist Shoji Tabuchi moved their acts to Branson. The flood of stars who have built theaters or perform regularly in Branson in the early 1990s include Mel Tillis, Ray Stevens, Moe Bandy, Jeannie Pruett, Buck Trent, Louise Mandrell, Glen Campbell, Andy Williams, the Gatlins, Johnny Cash, Willie Nelson, Merle Haggard, and Loretta Lynn.

Q. In 1958 who became a partner with Ted Daffan in a music publishing enterprise?

A. Hank Snow.

Q. Under what alias did Dick Curless produce a country music program on the Armed Forces Network during the Korean War?

A. The Rice Paddy Ranger.

Q. During 1976–77 what was the theme song of Dolly Parton's syndicated television show *Dolly*?

A. "Love Is like a Butterfly."

Q. What Norman Rockwell old-time cowboy character became a symbol of the country rock group Pure Prairie League?

A. Luke.

Q. Eddie Rabbitt provided the title track for what 1978 Clint Eastwood movie?

A. *Every Which Way but Loose.*

Q. In what year did TNN Viewer's Choice and the *Music City News* Country Awards merge?

A. 1990.

Q. Name the label which released the first charted records on Kenny Chesney.

A. Capricorn Records, noted also for finding the Allman Brothers, Wet Willie, and the Marshall Tucker Band.

Q. What is the title of the 1992 Reba McEntire biography written by Carl Leggett?

A. *Reba McEntire: The Queen of Country.*

———◆———

Q. What 1963 Boots Randolph hit became the theme song for *The Benny Hill Show*?

A. "Yakety Sax."

———◆———

Q. What role did Jerry Reed play in the short-lived 1977 CBS television series *Nashville 99*?

A. Detective Trace Mayne.

———◆———

Q. Prior to an ankle injury, Jim Reeves was signed for a short time to what major league baseball team?

A. The Saint Louis Cardinals.

———◆———

Q. On what network did *The Nashville Palace* air in 1981 and 1982?

A. NBC.

———◆———

Q. In what 1975 movie did Jerry Reed first work on-screen with Burt Reynolds?

A. *W. W. and the Dixie Dance Kings.*

———◆———

Q. Whose recordings, released under a variety of pseudonyms, sold approximately seventy-five million records during the 1920s, 1930s, and 1940s?

A. Vernon Dalhart.

Q. Who's left-handed, red-haired, Irish, produces Hal Ketchum, is a noted bluegrass artist, and has written two books—*Bossmen* and *Baby Let Me Follow You Down*?

A. Jim Rooney, who also managed Boston's famed folk group Mecca Club 47.

Q. What noted country picker-singer-songwriter appeared in the 1953 movie *From Here to Eternity*?

A. Merle Travis.

Q. In 1939 who became the first country music star to have a network radio program?

A. Red Foley.

Q. What is the title of Grandpa Jones's 1984 autobiography, cowritten with Charles Wolfe?

A. *Grandpa: Fifty Years behind the Mike.*

Q. Waylon Jennings appeared in what 1966 motion picture?

A. *Nashville Rebel.*

Q. Who claims to be the first country artist to have circled the globe on an international tour?

A. Little Jimmy Dickens.

Q. What country radio programing pioneer and announcer was known as the Solemn Ole Judge?

A. George D. Hay.

Q. Red Foley costarred with Fess Parker in what 1962–63 television series?

A. *Mr. Smith Goes to Washington.*

———◆———

Q. Who was the first singing cowboy for Warner Brothers?

A. Dick Foran (Nicholas Foran).

———◆———

Q. What Dallas facility was the home of *The Big D Jamboree?*

A. The Sportatorium.

———◆———

Q. In 1992 who became the first recipient of the ASCAP Voice of Music award?

A. Garth Brooks.

———◆———

Q. On what program hosted by Milton Berle did Eddy Arnold make his national television debut in 1949?

A. *Texaco Star Theater.*

———◆———

Q. Ernie Ashworth appeared in what 1965 movie?

A. *The Farmer's Other Daughter.*

———◆———

Q. What was the full title of the July–September 1973 television show that aired as *Music Country?*

A. *Dean Martin Presents Music Country.*

Called the King of Country Music, the late Roy Acuff first dreamed of becoming a professional baseball player until a series of sunstrokes forced him to pursue a different career. In the two years it took him to regain his health, he taught himself to play the fiddle, listening to the records of Fiddlin' John Carson and Gid Tanner and the Skillet Lickers. He learned to sing correctly — from the diaphragm — from his sister, a semi-professional light opera singer. A member of The Grand Ole Opry beginning in 1938, Roy believed that entertaining the audience was the highest form of his art. He picked up a yo-yo in 1931 at the corner drugstore and "never put it down," and learned to balance objects on his chin and nose in the fields as a young boy. "When I was living on the farm," he recalled, "like all farm boys and farm people, we entertained ourselves and our families. I used to take a corn stalk or something light, and I'd put it on my nose and try and balance it, if the wind would stop blowing long enough." He died in 1992.
[PHOTO COURTESY OF LES LEVERETT]

Q. Who hosted the 1970 musical variety program that served as a summer replacement for *The Andy Williams Show*?

A. Ray Stevens (*The Ray Stevens Show*).

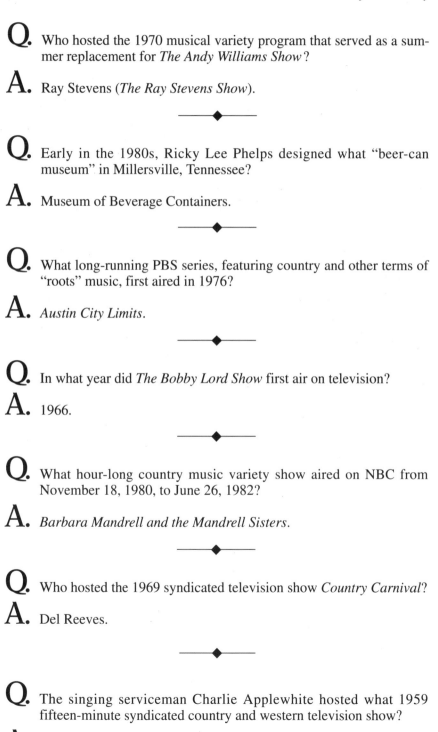

Q. Early in the 1980s, Ricky Lee Phelps designed what "beer-can museum" in Millersville, Tennessee?

A. Museum of Beverage Containers.

Q. What long-running PBS series, featuring country and other terms of "roots" music, first aired in 1976?

A. *Austin City Limits*.

Q. In what year did *The Bobby Lord Show* first air on television?

A. 1966.

Q. What hour-long country music variety show aired on NBC from November 18, 1980, to June 26, 1982?

A. *Barbara Mandrell and the Mandrell Sisters*.

Q. Who hosted the 1969 syndicated television show *Country Carnival*?

A. Del Reeves.

Q. The singing serviceman Charlie Applewhite hosted what 1959 fifteen-minute syndicated country and western television show?

A. *Country Style U.S.A.*

Q. Whose biography, entitled *One Day at a Time,* did Leland "Lee" Stoller and Peter Chaney write in 1983?

A. Cristy Lane.

Q. Who directed the syndicated television show *Eddy Arnold Time* produced in Springfield, Missouri?

A. Ben Park.

Q. What half-hour country and western television program was broadcast live from Springfield, Missouri, on NBC from March 17, 1961, to September 22, 1961?

A. *Five Star Jubilee.*

Q. In 1959 *The George Hamilton IV Show* on ABC originated in what city?

A. Washington, D.C.

Q. On what date did *Hee Haw* first air on CBS?

A. June 15, 1969.

Q. Before he had network shows, Jimmy Dean hosted a local show over what Washington, D.C., television station?

A. WTOP–TV.

Q. What is the seating capacity of the Grand Ole Opry House at Nashville's Opryland?

A. 4,400.

CMA Musician of the Year
(Changed from Instrumentalist of the Year in 1988)

1967	Chet Atkins	1982	Chet Atkins
1968	Chet Atkins	1983	Chet Atkins
1969	Chet Atkins	1984	Chet Atkins
1970	Jerry Reed	1985	Chet Atkins
1971	Jerry Reed	1986	Johnny Gimble
1972	Charlie McCoy	1987	Johnny Gimble
1973	Charlie McCoy	1988	Chet Atkins
1974	Don Rich	1989	Johnny Gimble
1975	Johnny Gimble	1990	Johnny Gimble
1976	Hargus "Pig" Robbins	1991	Mark O'Connor
1977	Roy Clark	1992	Mark O'Connor
1978	Roy Clark	1993	Mark O'Connor
1979	Charlie Daniels	1994	Mark O'Connor
1980	Roy Clark	1995	Mark O'Connor
1981	Chet Atkins		

Q. What new country label did Mercury Nashville spin off in 1994, with Toby Keith as it inaugural artist?

A. Polydor Records.

Q. Jerry Reed appeared in what 1976 Burt Reynolds movie?

A. *Gator.*

Q. What country music veteran ran unsuccessfully for the U.S. Senate from Tennessee in 1971?

A. Tex Ritter.

Q. Ed Bruce appeared in what 1979 television miniseries?

A. *The Chisholms.*

Q. Who founded the cable channel Country Music Television (CMT) in 1983?

A. Glenn Dean "Big Daddy" Daniels.

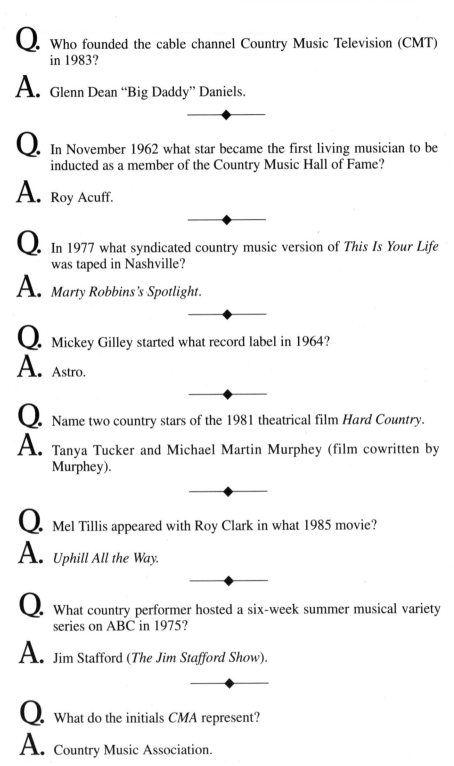

Q. In November 1962 what star became the first living musician to be inducted as a member of the Country Music Hall of Fame?

A. Roy Acuff.

Q. In 1977 what syndicated country music version of *This Is Your Life* was taped in Nashville?

A. *Marty Robbins's Spotlight.*

Q. Mickey Gilley started what record label in 1964?

A. Astro.

Q. Name two country stars of the 1981 theatrical film *Hard Country*.

A. Tanya Tucker and Michael Martin Murphey (film cowritten by Murphey).

Q. Mel Tillis appeared with Roy Clark in what 1985 movie?

A. *Uphill All the Way.*

Q. What country performer hosted a six-week summer musical variety series on ABC in 1975?

A. Jim Stafford (*The Jim Stafford Show*).

Q. What do the initials *CMA* represent?

A. Country Music Association.

Q. Scenes for what 1980 movie starring John Travolta were shot at Gilley's in Pasadena, Texas?

A. *Urban Cowboy.*

———◆———

Q. Where was the 1970 NBC summer replacement program *The Ray Stevens Show* taped?

A. Toronto, Canada.

———◆———

Q. Who designed the first electronic pickup to amplify a bass?

A. Everett Hull.

———◆———

Q. In what 1977 movie did Jerry Reed play a happy-go-lucky boot-legger?

A. *Smokey and the Bandit.*

———◆———

Q. Who rode into a *Hee Haw* audition on a six-foot-high unicycle?

A. Zella Lehr.

———◆———

Q. Johnny Lee had a spot in what 1979 made-for-television movie starring Barbara Eden and Susan St. James?

A. *The Girls in the Office.*

———◆———

Q. Who wrote the biography *George Jones: The Saga of an American Singer*?

A. Bob Allen.

Q. Which war-torn nation did singers Mark Collie and Lisa Stewart visit in 1996?

A. Bosnia.

Q. In 1958 Ferlin Husky had a part in what movie starring Zsa Zsa Gabor and Rocky Graziano?

A. *Country Music Holiday.*

Q. What businessman established the Prairie Dust label in 1976?

A. Sam Kirkpatrick.

Q. David Houston had a part in what 1967 movie?

A. *Cottonpickin' Chickenpickers.*

Q. In Nashville what was the first country music publisher to print its own sheet music?

A. Acuff–Rose.

Q. *Your Singing Fisherman* was the title of a 1983 biography of what performer?

A. Johnny Horton.

Q. Before its name was changed in 1927, what was *The Grand Ole Opry* called?

A. *The WSM Barn Dance* (*Saturday Night Barn Dance*).

Q. George Hamilton IV hosted what Canadian television program for five years?

A. *North Country.*

Q. In 1994 Wynonna and Naomi Judd parted ways with what longtime manager?

A. Ken Stilts.

———◆———

Q. Who built the successful publishing company of Jack Music?

A. Jack Clement.

———◆———

Q. Who named *The Grand Ole Opry* radio show on December 10, 1927?

A. George D. Hay.

———◆———

Q. *Pat Garrett and Billy the Kid, Alice Doesn't Live Here Anymore,* and *A Star Is Born* are among the movie credits of what country-rock singer-songwriter?

A. Kris Kristofferson.

———◆———

Q. Who produced Buddy Holly's first professional country session in Nashville for Decca Records in early 1956?

A. Owen Bradley.

———◆———

Q. In 1977 what became the number-one-rated non-network television show in the nation?

A. *Hee Haw.*

———◆———

Q. What prominent ASCAP executive has also been a hit Canadian producer, a successful publisher, and the writer of several hit songs, such as "Half the Way"?

A. English-born Ralph Murphy.

Opryland—The Home of American Music

Designed and built by the National Life and Accident Insurance Company (the original owners of Nashville radio station WSM and *The Grand Ole Opry*), Opryland USA is one of the most popular theme parks in the United States. Covering more than *one hundred acres* of rolling Tennessee countryside along the Cumberland River near Nashville, the park was developed to celebrate and showcase American music.

In addition to the musical productions, for which a yearly talent search across the United States brings hundreds of performers to Nashville, Opryland's attractions include high-tech roller coasters and water rides, restaurants and gift shops, sidewalk artists, animal and magic shows, game areas, a railroad, and a sky ride.

The groundbreaking for Opryland was in June 1970, and the park was opened in May 1972. In 1974 *The Grand Ole Opry* moved from its home of twenty-one years at the Ryman Auditorium to the new Opry House in the park. A circle of wood from the old Ryman stage was removed and inlaid into the new Opry stage as a symbol of the continuum of the music and the people who had made it. The Opryland Hotel was built in 1977 and the *General Jackson* showboat was acquired in 1985. The entire Opryland complex, and all of its subsidiary enterprises, was purchased by Gaylord Productions in 1983.

Q. Who won an Academy Award for portraying Loretta Lynn in the 1980 motion picture *Coal Miner's Daughter*?

A. Sissy Spacek.

———◆———

Q. Where was super-hit songwriter Kostas born?

A. Greece.

Q. What facility was the home of *The Louisiana Hayride*?

A. The Shreveport Municipal Auditorium.

Q. Who costarred in the 1960s television series *Rawhide* as Pete Nolan?

A. Sheb Wooley.

Q. *ACM* stands for what West Coast country music organization?

A. Academy of Country Music.

Q. Who produced Bob Luman's last album, *Alive and Well,* in 1977?

A. Johnny Cash.

Q. Who cohosted the first *Grand Ole Opry* television show with Ernest Tubb?

A. Judy Lynn.

Q. What musical composed by Roger Miller opened on Broadway in 1985?

A. *Big River.*

Q. Lari White appeared as a manipulative celebrity photographer in what 1994 made-for-television movie?

A. *XXX's and OOO's.*

Q. Who was the host of the popular TNN television show *Nashville Now*?

A. Ralph Emery.

◆

Q. Name at least two popular country entertainers born on Christmas Day.

A. Barbara Mandrell, Steve Wariner, and Jimmy Buffett were all born on December 25.

◆

Q. What one-time member of the Westerners composed and performed the theme song for the 1960s television series *Petticoat Junction*?

A. Curt Massey.

◆

Q. Acuff–Rose, the music publishers, launched what record label?

A. Hickory Records.

◆

Q. Who was the voice of the strolling troubadour rooster in Walt Disney's *Robin Hood*?

A. Roger Miller.

◆

Q. In the 1930 motion picture *Wagon Master*, who became the first singing cowboy to sing on-screen?

A. Ken Maynard.

◆

Q. Buck and Tex Ann Nation are credited with pioneering what type of entertainment facility in 1934?

A. A country music park.

Q. Gaylord Entertainment opened what $7.5 million country music attraction in downtown Nashville in 1994?

A. The Wildhorse Saloon.

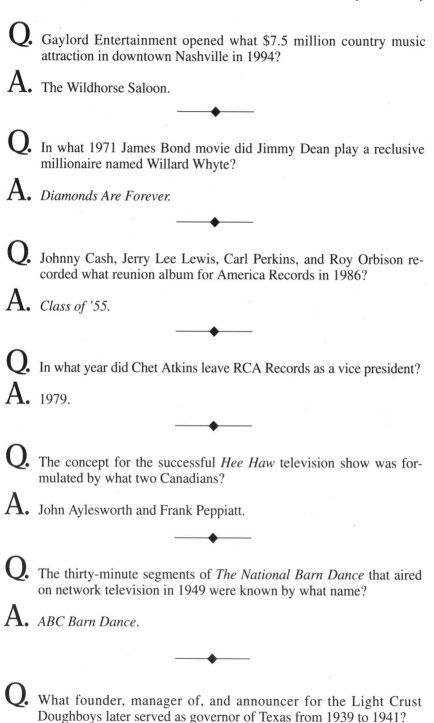

Q. In what 1971 James Bond movie did Jimmy Dean play a reclusive millionaire named Willard Whyte?

A. *Diamonds Are Forever.*

Q. Johnny Cash, Jerry Lee Lewis, Carl Perkins, and Roy Orbison recorded what reunion album for America Records in 1986?

A. *Class of '55.*

Q. In what year did Chet Atkins leave RCA Records as a vice president?

A. 1979.

Q. The concept for the successful *Hee Haw* television show was formulated by what two Canadians?

A. John Aylesworth and Frank Peppiatt.

Q. The thirty-minute segments of *The National Barn Dance* that aired on network television in 1949 were known by what name?

A. *ABC Barn Dance.*

Q. What founder, manager of, and announcer for the Light Crust Doughboys later served as governor of Texas from 1939 to 1941?

A. W. Lee "Pappy" O'Daniel.

Q. In what 1982 movie did Dolly Parton play a big-hearted madam in a bordello called the Chicken Ranch?

A. *The Best Little Whorehouse in Texas.*

Q. Charley Pride worked at a zinc-smelting plant in Helena, Montana, while playing semipro baseball with the East Helena Smelterites in what league?

A. Pioneer League.

Q. Joe Diffie, Kathy Mattea, Janie Fricke, and Jeff Carson were all discovered performing what Music Row activity?

A. All were "demo" singers making initial recordings of new songs.

Q. What was the first country music video to be shot in Rome, Italy?

A. Lari White's *What a Woman Wants.*

Q. What television show did Mel Street have in Bluefield, West Virginia?

A. *Country Showcase.*

Q. In what Clint Eastwood movie did Merle Travis make his last screen appearance?

A. *Honky-Tonk Man.*

Q. In 1941 Ernest Tubb appeared in what Columbia motion picture?

A. *Fightin' Buckaroos.*

Q. On what Montgomery, Alabama, radio station did Hank Williams perform intermittently for over a decade?

A. WSFA.

Q. What country and pop singer appeared in such movies as *Sex Kittens Go to College, Platinum High School,* and *College Confidential?*

A. Conway Twitty.

Q. What professional baseball club turned down Charley Pride in 1962?

A. New York Mets.

Q. What country comic has written such books as *Ain't God Good, Life EverLaughter,* and *Stories from Home?*

A. Jerry Clower.

Q. Name the only U.S. senator to have a hit country single.

A. Illinois senator Everett McKinley Dirksen (reached number fifty-eight on the charts with "Gallant Men" in 1967).

Q. What two hit singles by Kenny Rogers led to made-for-television movies with the same titles?

A. "The Gambler" and "Coward of the County."

Q. What *Hee Haw* cast member became Kenny Rogers's fourth wife?

A. Marianne Gordon.

Q. On what syndicated television talent contest show did Sawyer Brown come to national attention in 1984?

A. *Star Search.*

◆

Q. Before entering country music, John Schneider played what character on the CBS television series *The Dukes of Hazzard*?

A. Bo Duke.

◆

Q. Known for her novelty hillbilly numbers, Dorothy Shay appeared in what 1951 Abbott and Costello movie?

A. *Comin' 'round the Mountain.*

◆

Q. Name Willie Nelson's wives.

A. Martha Matthews, Shirley Collie, Connie Jean Koepke, and Annie d'Angelo.

◆

Q. Who produced T. G. Sheppard's 1979 number-one hits "Last Cheater's Waltz" and "I'll Be Coming Back for More"?

A. Buddy Killen.

◆

Q. Carl Smith had what network television show in Canada that was syndicated to stations in the United States?

A. *Carl Smith's Country Music Hall.*

◆

Q. What were the official trading cards of the West Coast-based ACM?

A. Country Classic.

Q. Leroy Van Dyke made his screen debut in what 1967 film?

A. *What Am I Bid?*

------◆------

Q. What African American country singers have had Top-30 singles?

A. Charley Pride, Ray Charles, Big Al Downing, Stoney Edwards, and Linda Martell.

------◆------

Q. Who were the original cohosts of the television series *Hee Haw*?

A. Buck Owens and Roy Clark.

------◆------

Q. *The Jimmy Dean Show* regularly featured what Jim Henson puppet creation?

A. Rowlf (the dog).

------◆------

Q. Kitty Wells created the name of what record label from the names of her children, Ruby, Bobby, and Carol Sue?

A. Ruboca Records.

------◆------

Q. What 1973 Dottie West hit, which she also wrote, was adapted into a Coca-Cola commercial?

A. "Country Sunshine."

------◆------

Q. How long did Tom Wopat last as host of TNN's *Prime Time Country*?

A. Just over three months.

Q. In 1985 what organization purchased the Acuff–Rose music catalog containing some twenty thousand copyrights?

A. Opryland USA (Opryland Music Group).

———◆———

Q. What is the name of Tim McGraw's management operation?

A. Breakfast Table Management.

———◆———

Q. Where in Illinois was Willie Nelson's first Farm Aid concert held in 1985?

A. Champaign.

———◆———

Q. Who was cohost with Tex Ritter during the 1930s on the *WHN Barn Dance* in New York?

A. Ray Whitley.

———◆———

Q. During 1978–79 what half-hour syndicated television sitcom was a spin-off from *Hee Haw*?

A. *Hee Haw Honeys.*

———◆———

Q. Because of the proliferation of country music in the area, what South Carolina resort city has been called Branson-by-the-Sea?

A. Myrtle Beach.

———◆———

Q. Country pop singer-songwriter Matraca Berg had a small role in what Timothy Hutton movie?

A. *Made in Heaven.*

Q. What program was the 1972 replacement on CBS for *The Glen Campbell Goodtime Hour*?

A. *The Jerry Reed When You're Hot You're Hot Hour.*

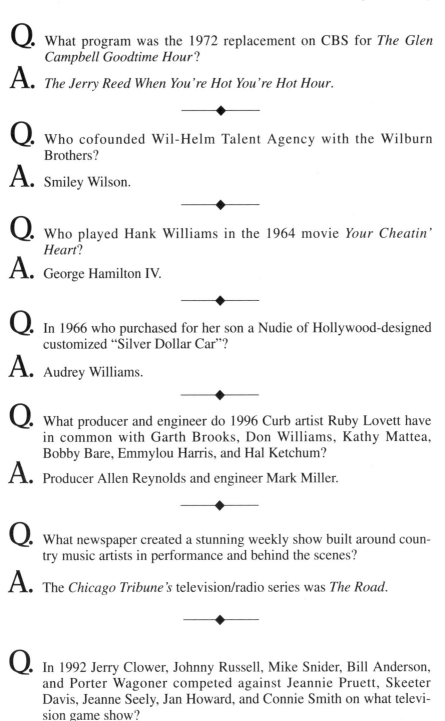

Q. Who cofounded Wil-Helm Talent Agency with the Wilburn Brothers?

A. Smiley Wilson.

Q. Who played Hank Williams in the 1964 movie *Your Cheatin' Heart*?

A. George Hamilton IV.

Q. In 1966 who purchased for her son a Nudie of Hollywood-designed customized "Silver Dollar Car"?

A. Audrey Williams.

Q. What producer and engineer do 1996 Curb artist Ruby Lovett have in common with Garth Brooks, Don Williams, Kathy Mattea, Bobby Bare, Emmylou Harris, and Hal Ketchum?

A. Producer Allen Reynolds and engineer Mark Miller.

Q. What newspaper created a stunning weekly show built around country music artists in performance and behind the scenes?

A. The *Chicago Tribune's* television/radio series was *The Road.*

Q. In 1992 Jerry Clower, Johnny Russell, Mike Snider, Bill Anderson, and Porter Wagoner competed against Jeannie Pruett, Skeeter Davis, Jeanne Seely, Jan Howard, and Connie Smith on what television game show?

A. *Family Feud.*

Q. What price was paid by Steve Buckner of Wichita, Kansas, for two tickets and two backstage passes for an October 13, 1992, Garth Brooks concert?

A. $3,400.

Q. What country music organization is known for its "Hat Awards"?

A. Academy of Country Music.

Q. What country music publication did Minnie Pearl inaugurate on September 1, 1944?

A. *The Grinder's Switch Gazette.*

Q. In what year did the *Baldknobbers Hillbilly Jamboree Show* open in Branson, Missouri?

A. 1968.

Q. What two guest characters did Roy Clark play on the 1960s television series *The Beverly Hillbillies*?

A. Cousin Roy and Big Mama Halsey.

Q. How long did it take promoters to sell twenty-three thousand tickets to Garth Brooks's 1992 concerts in Tulsa and Oklahoma City?

A. Three hours.

Q. Charlie Daniels appeared in what 1986 made-for-television movie?

A. *Lone Star Kid.*

Q. What singer-songwriter wrote the novel *Psychopath*?

A. David Allan Coe.

Q. In 1992 what dance craze inspired by Billy Ray Cyrus's first video release swept country music clubs across America?

A. The Achy Breaky.

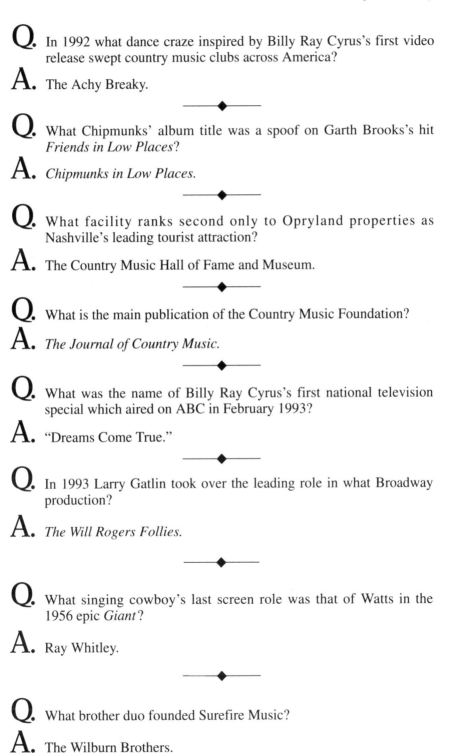

Q. What Chipmunks' album title was a spoof on Garth Brooks's hit *Friends in Low Places*?

A. *Chipmunks in Low Places.*

Q. What facility ranks second only to Opryland properties as Nashville's leading tourist attraction?

A. The Country Music Hall of Fame and Museum.

Q. What is the main publication of the Country Music Foundation?

A. *The Journal of Country Music.*

Q. What was the name of Billy Ray Cyrus's first national television special which aired on ABC in February 1993?

A. "Dreams Come True."

Q. In 1993 Larry Gatlin took over the leading role in what Broadway production?

A. *The Will Rogers Follies.*

Q. What singing cowboy's last screen role was that of Watts in the 1956 epic *Giant*?

A. Ray Whitley.

Q. What brother duo founded Surefire Music?

A. The Wilburn Brothers.

Fan Fair

The first annual International Country Music Fan Fair was held April 12–15, 1972, at Nashville's Municipal Auditorium. Five thousand fans attended, and more than one hundred artists, including Roy Acuff, Loretta Lynn, Bill Monroe, Jim and Jesse, Tom T. Hall, Ernest Tubb, Del Wood, Mac Wiseman, Lester Flatt, Wilma Lee and Stoney Cooper, and Pee Wee King, performed in excess of twenty hours of live entertainment. It sells out annually and now stretches over seven days.

The original premise of Fan Fair, co-sponsored by the Country Music Association and *The Grand Ole Opry*, was twofold: to relieve some of the congestion caused by the large number of people who converged on Nashville during the yearly October disk jockey convention; and to honor and entertain the fans of country music.

Described as "part concert, part family reunion, part religious experience," Fan Fair week includes stage shows, exhibit halls selling records and merchandise, photograph and autograph sessions, special meals, the Grand Master's Fiddling Contest, an auction of items donated by the stars, admittance to Opryland, the Country Music Hall of Fame and Museum, the Ryman Auditorium, and much more.

By 1996 one of the biggest-selling solo artists in America, Garth Brooks, still modestly claims, "I'm not a major talent. I'm a product of the people." He made music history in late 1991 when his third album, Ropin' the Wind, *debuted at number one on the* Billboard *pop charts, knocking his second album,* No Fences, *down to the number-two position. Troyal Garth Brooks, the youngest of six children, was born on February 7, 1962, and raised in Yukon, Oklahoma, on the outskirts of Oklahoma City. His mother, Colleen, also a country singer, recorded for Capitol Records and appeared on* The Ozark Jubilee *in the 1950s. Garth learned to play the guitar when he was a junior in high school, and while attending college at Oklahoma State on a partial athletic scholarship as a*

javelin thrower, he began performing as a solo act in night-clubs. He married Sandy Mahl in 1986 and moved to Nashville the following year. Outspoken about his family life and his music, Garth Brooks has revolutionized country music's public image and set a new standard for the industry's future prosperity. [PHOTO COURTESY OF ALAN MAYOR]

Q. What country great appeared in such movies as *Ballad of a Gunfighter, The Badge of Marshal Brennan,* and *Buffalo Gun?*

A. Marty Robbins.

Q. Who produced Vince Gill's first MCA album, *When I Call Your Name?*

A. Tony Brown.

Q. Audrey Williams formed what record label in 1968?

A. Bonanza Records.

Q. What whiskey-drinking killer did Sheb Wooley play in the 1952 movie *High Noon?*

A. Ben Miller.

Q. During the mid-1960s, what California city was often called Nashville West?

A. Bakersfield.

Q. Who played the role of Willy Moss in the 1960s television series *McHale's Navy?*

A. Bobby Wright.

Q. What nonprofit organization operates the Country Music Hall of Fame?

A. The Country Music Foundation.

Q. In 1958 Johnny Cash played a crazed killer in what B movie?

A. *Five Minutes to Live* (later retitled *Door to Door Maniac*).

———◆———

Q. In what 1969 movie did Glen Campbell costar with John Wayne?

A. *True Grit.*

———◆———

Q. In 1994 what record label was formed to capture on tape the annual Colorado Telluride Bluegrass Festival for consumers?

A. Blue Planet Records.

———◆———

Q. What singer-songwriter appeared in such westerns as *Nevada Smith* and *Five Card Stud*?

A. Merle Kilgore.

———◆———

Q. Who became Dot Records's country A&R director in 1957?

A. Mac Wiseman.

———◆———

Q. What was the title of Jan Howard's autobiography that was published in 1987?

A. *Sunshine and Shadow.*

———◆———

Q. Bobby Bare appeared in what western movie?

A. *A Distant Trumpet.*

———◆———

Q. For the taping of what 1993 CBS television special did Alan Jackson introduce his clean-shaven look?

A. "Country Music Celebration."

Q. Who costarred with Kenny Rogers and Travis Tritt in the 1993 CBS made-for-television movie *Rio Diablo*?

A. Naomi Judd.

◆

Q. The Judds, Chet Atkins, Crystal Gayle, and Barbara Mandrell are all recipients of what Nashville Symphony Association award?

A. The Harmony Award.

◆

Q. Who has written such children's books as *Runaway Thanksgiving* and *Jonathan's Gifts*?

A. Louise Mandrell.

◆

Q. What English journalist-author-compiler-publicist has championed the cause of country music in Europe since 1970?

A. Tony Byworth.

◆

Q. What cable television tribute to Minnie Pearl was the last show on which Roger Miller appeared?

A. "Hats off to Minnie."

◆

Q. Where in Indiana is the Bill Monroe Museum?

A. Bean Blossom.

◆

Q. Lorrie Morgan played a homicide detective in what 1994 television pilot?

A. *Loralei Lee*.

Q. When did *The Ozark Jubilee* television series go on the air?

A. January 22, 1955.

◆

Q. Where in Tennessee is Dolly Parton's Dollywood theme park?

A. Pigeon Forge.

◆

Q. Who produced or coproduced such country stars as John Berry, Reba McEntire, Hank Williams Jr., George Strait, Conway Twitty, Barbara Mandrell, Eddy Raven, Suzy Bogguss, and the Bellamy Brothers?

A. Nashville's Jimmy Bowen.

◆

Q. Which organization's annual awards show began first, the Academy of Country Music's (ACM) or the Country Music Association (CMA)?

A. The ACM began in 1967 and preceded the CMA Awards by one year.

◆

Q. What Nashville medical facility named its cancer treatment and research center in honor of Sarah Cannon (Minnie Pearl)?

A. Centennial Medical Center.

◆

Q. George Strait starred with Lesley Ann Warren in what 1992 motion picture?

A. *Pure Country.*

◆

Q. With what children's book did Ricky Van Shelton make his literary debut?

A. *Tales from a Duck Named Quacker.*

Q. For the first time, the Jerry Lewis Muscular Dystrophy Labor Day Telethon broadcast five hours of country programming in 1992 from what Branson, Missouri, facility?

A. Mel Tillis Theater.

Q. In 1992 President George Bush bestowed the prestigious Presidential National Medal of Arts on what two country music greats, who thus joined Roy Acuff, a previous recipient of the honor?

A. Minnie Pearl and Earl Scruggs.

Q. What year were the first Grammy Awards given?

A. Awards were first given in 1959 for recordings made in 1958.

Q. Who won the first Grammy Award in the country field?

A. The Kingston Trio's "Tom Dooley" was chosen for Best Country and Western Performance.

Q. At age thirteen Tanya Tucker had a cameo role in what motion picture?

A. *Jeremiah Johnson.*

Q. What Texas entrepreneur founded the Starday and Musicor record labels?

A. Harold W. "Pappy" Daily.

Q. In 1955 who built the quonset hut studio that served as the birthplace of Nashville's world-famous Music Row?

A. Owen and Harold Bradley.

CMA Video of the Year
   (Initiated in 1985, Not Awarded in 1988)

1985   "All My Rowdy Friends Are Comin' Over Tonight"/
         Hank Williams Jr./directed by John Goodhue/
         Warner Bros. Records

1986   "Who's Gonna Fill Their Shoes?"/George Jones/
         directed by Mark Ball/Epic Records

1987   "My Name Is Bocephus"/Hank Williams Jr./directed
         by Fisher Preaman/Warner Bros. Records

1989   "There's a Tear in My Beer"/Hank Williams Jr./
         Hank Williams Sr./directed by Ethan Russell/
         Warner Bros. Records

1990   "The Dance"/Garth Brooks/directed by John Lloyd
         Miller/Capitol Nashville

1991   "The Thunder Rolls"/Garth Brooks/directed by Bud
         Schaetzle/Capitol Nashville

1992   "Midnight In Montgomery"/Alan Jackson/directed
         by Jim Shea/Arista

1993   "Chattahoochee"/Alan Jackson/directed by Martin
         Kahan/Arista

1994   "Independence Day"/Martina McBride/directed by
         Robert Deaton and George J. Flanigen IV/RCA

1995   "Baby Likes to Rock It"/The Tractors/directed by
         Micheal Salomon/Arista

Q. Who hosted the *Ozark Jubilee* television series on ABC?

A. Red Foley.

———◆———

Q. Where in Kentucky is the International Bluegrass Music Association establishing a museum and Bluegrass Hall of Honor?

A. Owensboro.

———◆———

Q. In what year was *The Grand Ole Opry* inducted into the Radio Hall of Fame?

A. 1992.

Q. Ricky Van Shelton covered what Elvis Presley hit for the soundtrack of the motion picture *Honeymoon in Vegas*?

A. "Wear My Ring around Your Neck."

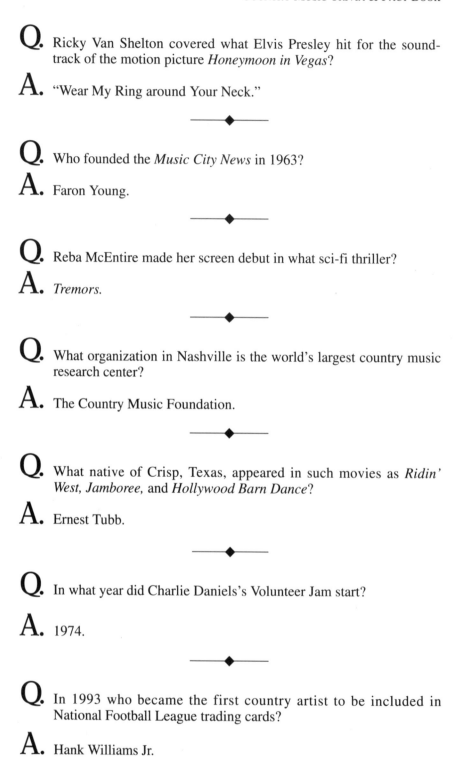

Q. Who founded the *Music City News* in 1963?

A. Faron Young.

Q. Reba McEntire made her screen debut in what sci-fi thriller?

A. *Tremors.*

Q. What organization in Nashville is the world's largest country music research center?

A. The Country Music Foundation.

Q. What native of Crisp, Texas, appeared in such movies as *Ridin' West, Jamboree,* and *Hollywood Barn Dance*?

A. Ernest Tubb.

Q. In what year did Charlie Daniels's Volunteer Jam start?

A. 1974.

Q. In 1993 who became the first country artist to be included in National Football League trading cards?

A. Hank Williams Jr.

The Nashville Network (TNN)

Before cable television's The Nashville Network (TNN) debuted on March 7, 1983, country music artists relied almost entirely on touring and radio airplay to sell their records. This often made the task of reaching larger and more diverse audiences difficult. Now one of cable's most-watched networks, TNN (part of the Opryland corporate complex) has grown from an initial seven million subscribers to over sixty million throughout the United States and Canada, and from its original twelve programs in 1983 to more than fifty today.

Some of TNN's historical highlights include:

March 1984: First country music video show on television, "Country Clips," airs starring hosts Steve Hall and Shotgun Red.

April 1985: For the first time in its nearly sixty-year history, *The Grand Ole Opry* radio show is made available live to TV viewers on a weekly basis.

July 1987: TNN household subscribers exceed thirty-five million.

November 1987: TNN becomes the official network of the USO.

March 1988: First Viewer's Choice Awards Show, now the TNN-MCN *(Music City News)* Country Awards broadcasts.

March 1991: First broadcast of a live NASCAR race.

Q. What trio had a weekly children's series on CBS?

A. Riders in the Sky.

◆

Q. Who produced Tennessee Ernie Ford's 1962–65 ABC network television show?

A. William Burch.

```
CMA Comedian of the Year
(Discontinued in 1971)

1967   Don Bowman        1969   Archie Campbell
1968   Ben Colder        1970   Roy Clark
```

Q. During what years was *The Wilburn Brothers Show* produced for syndication?

A. 1963–1974.

———◆———

Q. A session with what artist in 1962 launched Jerry Kennedy's producing career?

A. Rex Allen.

———◆———

Q. Scott Faragher wrote what book about greed and backstabbing within the country music business in Nashville?

A. *Music City Babylon.*

———◆———

Q. The CMA Awards have been given since 1968. Name the only two independent label artists as of 1996 to win for "Single of the Year."

A. Jeannie C. Riley and Alison Krauss.

———◆———

Q. Whose popular autobiography is entitled *Memories*?

A. Ralph Emery.

———◆———

Q. Who formed the giant Cedarwood music publishing company?

A. James R. Denny and Webb Pierce.

Q. What Dallas version of Nashville's Fan Fair was held from 1992 to 1994?

A. Fan Jam.

—————◆—————

Q. How were Airborne Records and Imprint Records (originally Veritas Records) funded.

A. By public stock offerings.

—————◆—————

Q. Who pioneered and promoted usage of the term *country music*?

A. Connie B. Gay.

—————◆—————

Q. In what year did Grant Turner, who became known as the Dean of Opry Announcers, first begin working at *The Grand Ole Opry*?

A. 1945.

—————◆—————

Q. What Fort Worth, Texas, country music honky-tonk is considered the world's largest nightspot?

A. Billy Bob's Texas.

—————◆—————

Q. What Hank Williams Jr. biography was made into an NBC television movie starring Richard Thomas?

A. *Living Proof.*

—————◆—————

Q. What is the title of Johnny Cash's autobiography that has been translated into nine languages?

A. *The Man in Black.*

Q. What Texas dancehall opened in Dallas in 1957 in the former home of Bob Wills's Ranch House?

A. The Longhorn Ballroom.

Q. What organization established the Songwriters Hall of Fame in 1970?

A. The Nashville Songwriters Association International.

Q. In 1972 who became the first American country artist to have his own television series in England?

A. George Hamilton IV.

Q. What awards designated by fans were first presented in 1966?

A. *Music City News* Awards (now TNN/*Music City News* Country Awards).

Q. On what date did Nashville's Opryland USA music theme park open?

A. May 27, 1972.

Q. Airing on September 12, 1981, what was the first cable television show to be broadcast from Nashville?

A. *Nashville Alive.*

Q. What was the first year that the CMA Awards were broadcast on network television?

A. 1968.

Q. When was the country music-oriented cable television service the Nashville Network (TNN) launched?

A. March 7, 1983.

——————◆——————

Q. At whose insistence was RCA's now-famous Studio B constructed in Nashville in 1957?

A. Chet Atkins.

——————◆——————

Q. What Oklahoma resident assembled and presented to Johnny Cash an automobile, made from parts of 1949 through 1973 Cadillacs, in honor of Cash's 1976 single "One Piece at a Time"?

A. Bill Patch.

——————◆——————

Q. What is the oldest country music publication in the United States?

A. *Country Song Roundup.*

——————◆——————

Q. What Nashville facility was the home of *The Grand Ole Opry* from 1943 to 1974?

A. The Ryman Auditorium.

——————◆——————

Q. Billy Dean had a supporting role in what short-lived television series?

A. *Elvis.*

——————◆——————

Q. The Discover credit card was conceived and developed by the father of what Atlantic recording artist?

A. Ray Kennedy.

Q. What label did Shelby Singleton found in 1968?

A. Plantation Records.

◆

Q. What singing cowboy went on to become the owner of the California Angels baseball team?

A. Gene Autry.

◆

Q. Roy Acuff tried out unsuccessfully with what East Tennessee baseball team?

A. The Knoxville Smokies.

◆

Q. What Dallas radio station aired *The Big D Jamboree* from 1947 through the early 1960s?

A. KRLD.

◆

Q. What producer-composer-vocalist is nicknamed Cowboy Jack?

A. Jack Clement.

◆

Q. To what publication did Hank Williams dedicate his composition "Moanin' the Blues"?

A. *Country Song Roundup.*

◆

Q. Col. Tom Parker managed what country artist from 1954 to 1956?

A. Hank Snow.

Q. What organization bestows the Golden Guitar Awards?

A. The Country Music Association of Australia.

———◆———

Q. Who played composer and publisher Fred Rose in the 1980 television special "Hank Williams: The Man and His Music"?

A. Henry Arnold.

———◆———

Q. Who wrote the theme song for the TNN series *I-40 Paradise*?

A. Lionel Cartwright.

———◆———

Q. Who bought Sun Records from founder Sam Phillips in 1969?

A. Shelby Singleton.

———◆———

Q. What was the title of Jimmie Rodgers Snow's 1977 autobiography?

A. *I Cannot Go Back.*

———◆———

Q. Begun in 1969 what's the longest-surviving overseas country music publication?

A. *Country Music People*, published in London.

———◆———

Q. What character in the play and movie *Bye Bye Birdie* satirized Conway Twitty?

A. Conrad Birdie.

———◆———

Q. Who was elected as the first president of the Country Music Association following its organization in 1958?

A. Connie B. Gay.

Following in Their Footsteps

Throughout country music history, many sons and daughters have accompanied or succeeded their famous parents into the spotlight. Some have equaled or even surpassed the family legacies. Following is a list of the most prominent of those parent-child combinations.

Roy Acuff Sr.—Roy Acuff Jr.
Rex Allen Sr. —Rex Allen Jr.
Liz Anderson—Lynn Anderson
Dr. Humphrey Bate—Buster Bate, Alcyone Bate
Pat Boone—Debby Boone
Cliff Carlisle— Tommy "Sonny Boy" Carlisle
"Mother" Maybelle Carter—June (Carter) Cash, Helen Carter, Anita Carter
June Carter and Carl Smith—Carlene Carter
Johnny Cash—Rosanne Cash, Cindy Cash, John Carter Cash
Cowboy Copas—Cathy Copas
Red Foley—Betty Foley
Merle Haggard—Marty Haggard
Theron Hale—Mamie Ruth and Elizabeth Hale
George Hamilton IV—George "Hege" Hamilton V
Naomi Judd—Wynonna Judd
Royce Kendall—Jeannie Kendall
Uncle Dave Macon—Dorris Macon
George Morgan—Lorrie Morgan
Buck Owens—Buddy Alan (Alvis Alan Owens)
Don Reno—Ronnie Reno, Don Wayne Reno, Dale Reno
Marty Robbins—Ronny Robbins
Roy Rogers Sr.—Roy "Dusty" Rogers Jr.
Earl Scruggs—Randy, Gary, and Steve Scruggs
Asher Sizemore—"Little" Jimmy Sizemore
Hank Snow—Rev. Jimmie Rodgers Snow
Mel Tillis—Pam Tillis
Calvin Tubb—Glenn Douglas (Tubb), Bill Talmadge (Tubb)
Ernest Tubb—Justin Tubb
Conway Twitty—Michael (Charlie Tango), Joani Lee, Kathy
Doc Watson—Merle Watson
Kitty Wells and Johnny Wright—Bobby Wright, Ruby Wright
Dottie West—Shelly West
Buck White—Sharon (White) Skaggs, Cheryl White, Rosie White
Slim Whitman—Byron Whitman
Hank Williams Sr.—Hank Williams Jr. and Jett Williams

Johnny Cash, the son of cotton sharecroppers, was born on February 26, 1932, in Kingsland, Arkansas. Like many of his contemporaries, including Willie Nelson and Waylon Jennings, Johnny turned to music as a means toward achieving a dream of a better life. He married his first wife, Vivian Liberto, the mother of his four daughters, in the early 1950s. They settled in Memphis, where he recorded his first songs for Sam Phillips's Sun Records in 1955. Rosanne was born on May 24, 1955, and her parents separated in the early 1960s, but she and her father always stayed in touch. In late 1987, Rosanne's "Tennessee Flat Top Box" debuted on the Billboard charts, eventually reaching number one. The song had been number eleven on the chart for Johnny in 1962, but Rosanne did not know until afterwards that her father had written it as well as recorded it. "I had heard it since I was three years old and I just thought it was public domain. But Rodney [Crowell, her husband at the time] kept saying, 'I really think your dad wrote this.' But when I found out that he had, I really wasn't surprised. I thought, 'Of course he did! Who else could have written that?'" [PHOTO COURTESY OF ALAN MAYOR]

Q. Cincinnati's *Midwestern Hayride* was first known by what name?

A. *Boone County Jamboree.*

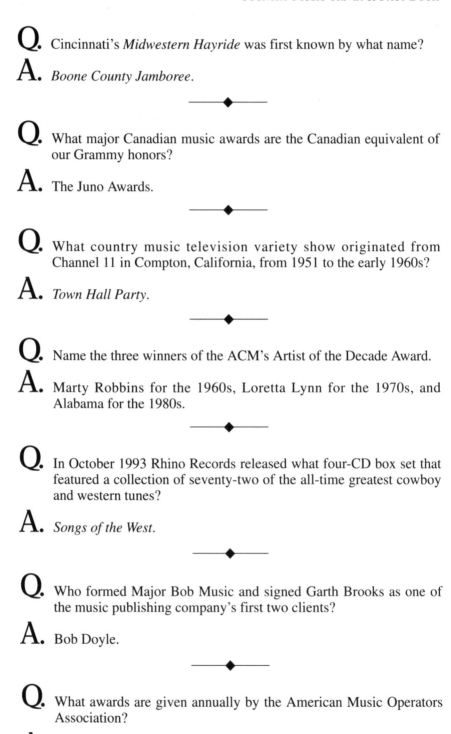

Q. What major Canadian music awards are the Canadian equivalent of our Grammy honors?

A. The Juno Awards.

Q. What country music television variety show originated from Channel 11 in Compton, California, from 1951 to the early 1960s?

A. *Town Hall Party.*

Q. Name the three winners of the ACM's Artist of the Decade Award.

A. Marty Robbins for the 1960s, Loretta Lynn for the 1970s, and Alabama for the 1980s.

Q. In October 1993 Rhino Records released what four-CD box set that featured a collection of seventy-two of the all-time greatest cowboy and western tunes?

A. *Songs of the West.*

Q. Who formed Major Bob Music and signed Garth Brooks as one of the music publishing company's first two clients?

A. Bob Doyle.

Q. What awards are given annually by the American Music Operators Association?

A. Jukebox Awards.

Q. What Georgia town hosts Alan Jackson Day?

A. Newnan.

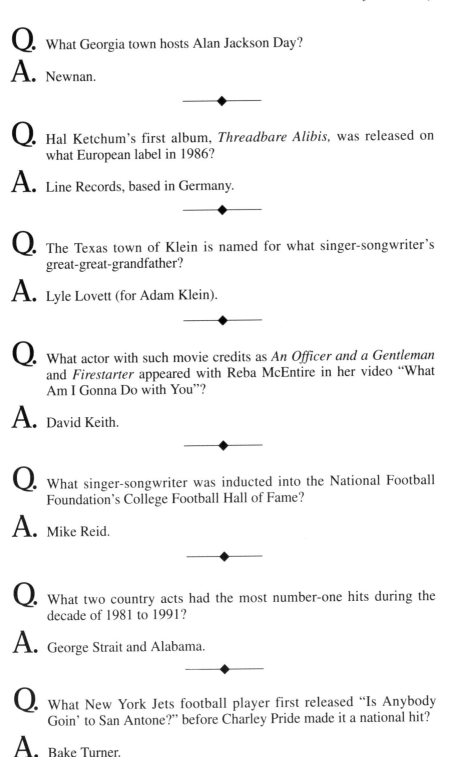

Q. Hal Ketchum's first album, *Threadbare Alibis,* was released on what European label in 1986?

A. Line Records, based in Germany.

Q. The Texas town of Klein is named for what singer-songwriter's great-great-grandfather?

A. Lyle Lovett (for Adam Klein).

Q. What actor with such movie credits as *An Officer and a Gentleman* and *Firestarter* appeared with Reba McEntire in her video "What Am I Gonna Do with You"?

A. David Keith.

Q. What singer-songwriter was inducted into the National Football Foundation's College Football Hall of Fame?

A. Mike Reid.

Q. What two country acts had the most number-one hits during the decade of 1981 to 1991?

A. George Strait and Alabama.

Q. What New York Jets football player first released "Is Anybody Goin' to San Antone?" before Charley Pride made it a national hit?

A. Bake Turner.

Sho-Bud Steel Guitars

One of the most renowned brands of pedal steel guitars had a humble beginning in Madison, Tennessee. In 1953 Harold B. "Shot" Jackson, while working with the duo of Johnny and Jack, lived in a mobile home behind Jack Anglin's home. Jack had a vacant chicken coop that Shot turned into a workshop and started repairing guitars and experimenting with attaching pedals to various brands of steel guitars.

In 1955, at the suggestion of *Grand Ole Opry* performer Jimmy Day, Shot started on a year-long project to construct the first steel guitar based on his own design. The second unit Shot built for his own use.

In 1957 Buddy Emmons started working with Shot. The first commercial model steel guitar constructed by Shot and Buddy was purchased by Don Warden, who was working with *The Porter Wagoner Show*. In addition to pedal steel guitars, Shot designed and constructed various custom flat-top guitars and dobros.

The company name of Sho-Bud was derived from the first three letters in the names of Shot Jackson and Buddy Emmons. Later Emmons left the firm and started his own steel guitar line and Sho-Bud became a part of the large instrument manufacturing conglomerate of Baldwin, Inc.

Q. Name the California restaurant and bar that was chosen Best Night Club by the ACM every year between 1986 and 1991.

A. Crazy Horse Steak House and Saloon in Santa Ana.

Q. What movie did Johnny Cash shoot with Kirk Douglas in 1970?

A. *The Gunfight.*

Q. What former piano player for such groups as the Oak Ridge Boys and the Stamps became president of MCA/Nashville in 1993?

A. Tony Brown.

During the late 1960s the Sho-Bud Gang performed extensively in the United States and abroad. (l to r) Jimmy Day; Shot Jackson; Donna Darlene (Shot's wife); Jack and Jerry, the Calhoun Twins. [PHOTO COURTESY OF DONNA JACKSON]

Q. Who was the first country performer to fill in for Johnny Carson on NBC's long-running *The Tonight Show*?

A. Roy Clark.

———◆———

Q. What tourist attraction did the late Conway Twitty open in Hendersonville, Tennessee, on June 6, 1982?

A. Music Village USA (Twitty City), now Heritage, U.S.A.

———◆———

Q. The initials *CCMA* stand for what country music organization?

A. Canadian Country Music Association.

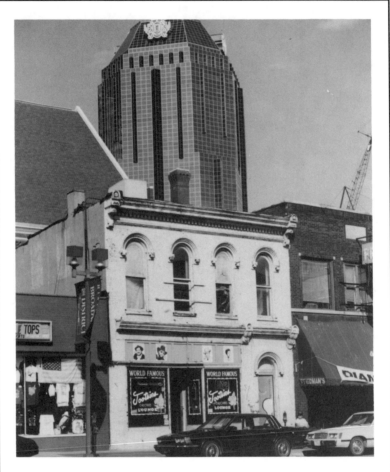

Tootsie's Orchid Lounge

Its back door opened into the alley directly across from the back door of the Ryman Auditorium, enabling *The Grand Ole Opry* stars to slip in for a beer or some of Tootsie's famous southern fried chicken between shows. Hattie Louise "Tootsie" Bess bought the old building on lower Broadway in March 1960 and ruled her domain with a compassion for pickers and singers down on their luck and a sharp hatpin in the rump for anyone whose behavior got out of hand. Willie Nelson, Tom T. Hall, Kris Kristofferson, and Roger Miller were some of her most famous regulars in the days before anyone even recognized their names. Previously, the club was called Mom's, and was owned by John and Louise "Mom" Hackler.

Country Weekly

Inaugural issue: April 12, 1994
Lead story: photo/journalistic story of Garth Brooks
Front page: photo of Garth Brooks with photo insets
of Randy Travis and Mary Chapin Carpenter
Other features:
 ■ "Randy Travis: I'm Back"
 ■ "Mary Chapin Carpenter: a Rare and
   personal Interview"
 ■ "Faith Hill: from Secretary to Superstar"
 ■ Interviews with Kitty Wells and Confederate
   Railroad's Danny Shirley
Single-copy cost: U.S. $1.49, Canada $1.79.
Initial press run: 750,000 copies with over 125 color
   photos of country music stars

Q. What 1929 movie short was Jimmie Rodgers's only screen appearance?

A. *The Singing Brakeman.*

———◆———

Q. In 1967 what became the first country music theater to open in Branson, Missouri?

A. Presleys' Mountain Music Jubilee.

Ernie Couch, his wife, Jill, and son, Jason, have been residents of Nashville since 1974. Ernie owns and operates Consultx, a support firm for the publishing industry with specialties in advertising and graphic design. Since 1985 Ernie and Jill have compiled about twenty trivia books for Rutledge Hill Press.